Aquatic Rescue and Safety

Dennis K. Graver

Human Kinetics

Library of Congress Cataloging-in-Publication Data

Graver, Dennis.
   Aquatic rescue and safety
water-related injuries / Dennis K. Graver.
      p. cm.
Includes bibliographical references and index.
  ISBN 0-7360-4122-2 (Soft Cover)
1. Aquatic sports--Safety measures. 2. Lifesaving. I. Title.
  GV770.6.G73 2003
  797'.028'9--dc21   2003008727

ISBN: 0-7360-4122-2

Acquisitions Editor: Amy N. Clocksin; **Developmental Editor:** Judy Park; **Assistant Editor:** Lee Alexander; **Copyeditor:** Patsy Fortney; **Proofreader:** Sue Fetters; **Indexer:** Bobbi Swanson; **Permission Manager:** Dalene Reeder; **Graphic Designer:** Fred Starbird; **Graphic Artist:** Yvonne Griffith and Denise Lowry; **Photo Manager:** Kareema McLendon; **Cover Designer:** Keith Blomberg; **Photographer (cover):** Raw Talent Photo; **Photographer (interior):** Dennis K. Graver, unless otherwise noted; **Art Manager:** Kelly Hendren; **Illustrator:** Hardlines Ltd. unless otherwise noted. Figure 6.2 by Argosy. Figures 4.15 and 4.16 by Thomas – Bradley Illustration and Design; **Printer:** United Graphics

The author would like to thank his photograph models: Bill Bothel, Jeff Ellingsen, Bob Lew, Mark Palmer, Jim Reinhardt, Ryan Shaughnessy, Robert Shelley, Darryl Tedrow, Trisha Teig, and Will Webb.

Printed in the United States of America   10 9 8 7 6 5 4 3 2 1

Human Kinetics
Web site: www.HumanKinetics.com

United States: Human Kinetics, P.O. Box 5076, Champaign, IL 61825-5076
800-747-4457
e-mail: humank@hkusa.com

Canada: Human Kinetics, 475 Devonshire Road Unit 100, Windsor, ON N8Y 2L5
800-465-7301 (in Canada only)
e-mail: orders@hkcanada.com

Europe: Human Kinetics, 107 Bradford Road, Stanningley, Leeds LS28 6AT, United Kingdom
+44 (0) 113 255 5665
e-mail: hk@hkeurope.com

Australia: Human Kinetics, 57A Price Avenue, Lower Mitcham, South Australia 5062
08 8277 1555
e-mail: liahka@senet.com.au

New Zealand: Human Kinetics, P.O. Box 105-231, Auckland Central
09-523-3462
e-mail: hkp@ihug.co.nz

Contents

Preface

Water covers more than 70 percent of the earth's surface. We bathe in the liquid and play in it, but water also causes fatalities. Swimming, boating, sailing, water skiing, rowing, canoeing, surfing, snorkeling, scuba diving, and other aquatic recreational activities are enjoyable, but can lead to drowning. Professional rescuers are called to respond to aquatic emergencies, but anyone who is near water also may be called upon to respond because it may be too late by the time professional rescuers arrive. This book is intended for anyone who may have to provide assistance—layperson or professional.

When we are warm, water is cooling, but the great capacity of water to absorb heat can result in excessive chilling, incapacitation, and even death. By the same token, water can warm us when we are cold, but water that is too hot can scald and cause life-threatening illness.

Many of us exercise in, on, and around water to keep ourselves healthy, but water can quickly exhaust seemingly healthy people and cause severe pulmonary and circulatory distress. Although water can be wonderful when we can immerse ourselves in it safely, the same liquid can be horrifying when it leads to injury or death.

There are many misconceptions about aquatic rescue techniques and emergency medical procedures. One of the primary purposes of this book is to provide both citizen and professional rescuers the latest rescue, first aid, and medical procedures—ones that have proven to be effective. Other major purposes for this book include identifying the causes of submersion injuries and minimizing accidents by prevention. Any accidents prevented by the application of the procedures presented in this book will have made the effort required to produce this work extremely worthwhile.

In the subtitle of this book I use the term *water-related injuries*. The dictionary defines an injury as "damage or loss sustained, esp. to a bodily part." Some of the difficulties caused by submersion may be classified as illnesses, which the dictionary defines as "the state or period of being ill" (*ill* meaning "of unsound physical or mental health"). For simplicity, we will consider illnesses, such as hypothermia, to be injuries throughout this book. There is no question that severe hypothermia or other serious illnesses can injure a body part.

As a scuba diving instructor for 35 years and as a medical services officer for a fire district, I have seen many emergencies, but water-related emergencies are unique because of the environment. Firefighters and other professionals must complete specialized training to qualify as responders for water rescues. Even swimming pool lifeguards must have additional training for rescues that take place in oceans, lakes, rivers, and other open water sites. This book provides valuable information about water rescues for everyone. Whether you are simply a boater or swimmer or are a member of a water rescue team, you will benefit from the information in this work, which was amassed over years of experience and training.

This book is divided into four parts. The first part pertains to the primary water-related emergency—drowning. The second part addresses the physiological considerations related to water emergencies, such as body temperature changes and head and spinal cord injuries. The chapters in part III concern specific injuries, such as those sustained while swimming and scuba diving. The fourth part includes information about first aid, evacuations, emergency action plans, and legal concerns. The book may be used as a text for water rescue training, as a resource for individual lessons, or as a reference for emergency preparedness.

While you read and study this book, I encourage the following approach: First, read the parts of the book that apply to your circumstances. If you or your family or friends do not scuba dive, you may choose to skip the chapter about scuba diving injuries. Second, determine what actions you need to take to be prepared to manage the aquatic emergencies that you are likely to encounter. Third, and most important, set a date to complete the required actions and prepare a schedule to accomplish your goal. You will need to complete training, obtain equipment, prepare emergency plans, and practice implementing your plans in the environment in which you are likely to need them. This approach is appropriate for both citizens and professional rescuers.

I have taught water rescue techniques for decades and have read many articles and books on the subject. In this book I have chosen to use my personal stories of water rescues as a springboard to help you learn effective rescue techniques. Stories are easy to remember, and when you can recall the story, it will help you remember the related principle.

Many people participate in aquatic recreation without giving careful thought to what they should do if something goes wrong. When an accident occurs, people without proper training or equipment often perish when they attempt to rescue loved ones. Even trained rescuers are injured or killed when they attempt heroic rescues. I want desperately for anyone who is in the vicinity of water to learn how to prevent and manage aquatic accidents. I am grateful for the opportunity to author this book because I am confident that the information it contains can help all who are interested in saving lives.

Part I

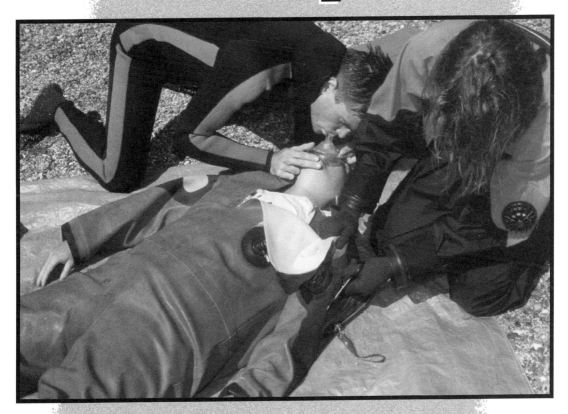

Introduction to Aquatic Rescue and Safety

Chapter 1

© Human Kinetics

Drowning

Few people experience such an emergency, but a submersion accident can occur anywhere there is water. You need to know what to look for, what to do, and what not to do if an aquatic emergency arises.

THERE WAS OBVIOUS ANXIETY in the divemaster's voice as he shouted, "Dennis, Dennis, Dennis!" My wife, our neighbors, and I were aboard a scuba diving charter boat in Cozumel, Mexico. We were in Cozumel for a scuba diving vacation, not for business purposes. I moved quickly to the front of the vessel and saw a scuba diver floating face down and motionless at the surface and another divemaster approaching him in the water. The divemaster turned the diver face up and, when he discovered the ghastly appearance of the victim, retreated instantly.

I donned my fins quickly, grabbed my rescue breathing mask, and jumped into the water. The boat had continued moving forward, so I was able to jump in right beside the victim. I opened his airway, drained water from his mouth, and gave him two rescue breaths through the rescue breathing mask. I listened again for breathing, and the victim made moaning sounds. With assistance from divers aboard the boat, we rapidly removed him from the water. I removed my fins, climbed aboard, and began caring for the victim.

The boat's emergency oxygen delivery system had an empty cylinder, so we had to rendezvous with another vessel and obtain an oxygen cylinder while en route to shore. We also were able to rendezvous with a speedboat and transfer the patient to the faster boat for a quicker trip to the beach. The charter boat captain used the boat's radio to summon an ambulance from town. Two other divers and I loaded the victim into the ambulance and followed it to town in a taxicab. The victim regained consciousness in the ambulance and was taken to a medical clinic for observation.

When I learned that the patient was in a medical clinic instead of a hospital, I went immediately to the facility, explained that the victim had lost consciousness while submerged, and insisted that he be transferred to a hospital immediately. To my relief, the medical technician listened to me. The patient was reloaded into the ambulance and taken to the local hospital emergency room. I followed again and used an interpreter to explain to the doctors what had happened.

Lung X rays detected a significant amount of water in the victim's right lung. The patient remained in the hospital under medical care for two days, flew home, and recovered completely from the incident. I shudder to think what might have happened if he had not received prompt medical treatment.

Learning Goals *By the end of this chapter, you should be able to:*

- ▶ Define the terms drowning, near drowning, submersion injury, aspiration syndrome, suffocation, postimmersion syndrome, and immersion syndrome.
- ▶ Describe the effects of the aspiration syndrome, suffocation during immersion, the postimmersion syndrome, and the immersion syndrome.
- ▶ Describe the physiology of the drowning process.
- ▶ Contrast desired and instinctive aquatic actions.
- ▶ List several actions each to prevent child, teenage, and adult drownings.

Definitions

Notice that I did not use the term *near drowning* in my introductory story. In recent years controversy has surrounded submersion injury terminology. The American Heart Association states that "*Drowning* refers to submersion events

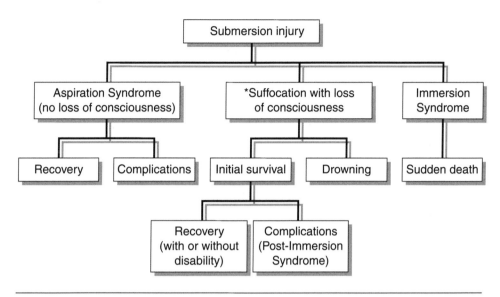

Figure 1.1 Submersion injury outcomes.
*With or without aspiration.

in which the victim is pronounced dead at the scene of attempted resuscitation (American Heart Association 2000, 233). Because drowning is terminal, the term cannot be used in relation to those who survive submersion injuries. *Near drowning*—a popular term for many years—has been used to describe submersion victims who survive for at least 24 hours. But if a victim aspirates liquid while submerged, lives more than 24 hours, and then dies from complications caused by the initial event, death remains drowning-related." The same American Heart Association source recommends that "the term *near-drowning* no longer be used. . . . Up until the time of drowning-related death, refer to the victim as a *submersion victim*." We will use the new and correct term of *submersion victim* throughout this book.

The definitions and possible outcomes of submersion injuries are summarized in figure 1.1. Three main scenarios may occur with a submersion injury: aspiration without loss of consciousness, suffocation with loss of consciousness, or immersion syndrome.

Aspiration Syndrome refers to the effects of aspiration of fluid into the lungs without loss of consciousness (Edmonds 1998). This may occur when a swimmer is attempting to breathe while in rough water or when a scuba diver has a leaking scuba regulator. After the accident the victim will have an immediate cough. After a short interval, the signs and symptoms listed in figure 1.2 may appear.

Aspiration Syndrome can lead to serious complications, including pulmonary edema (an accumulation of fluid in the lungs that reduces the ability to get

After a short interval, these signs and symptoms of Aspiration Syndrome may appear:

- Difficulty breathing
- Chest pain
- Pale or bluish skin color
- Shivering

Figure 1.2   Aspiration Syndrome.

oxygen into the bloodstream), pulmonary infection, and pneumonia. Medical attention is essential.

Suffocation is cessation of breathing leading to unconsciousness or death. Suffocation while immersed may or may not involve the aspiration of water. *"Wet" drowning* is a term used to classify a submersion injury involving the aspiration of water into the lungs. Literature claims this condition exists in 80 to 90 percent of all incidents (Modell 1976). *"Dry" drowning* is a controversial term referring to death caused by lack of oxygen because the victim's throat is locked shut by a tight closure of the vocal cords. The process is called a laryngeal spasm. Doctors, including Carl Edmonds and Chris Dueker, contest the concept because the vocal cords relax when body oxygen levels are low (Dueker 1999; Edmonds 1998). The chances of survival are much greater for a victim rescued before laryngeal spasm ceases than they are for a wet-drowning victim.

Secondary drowning and *delayed drowning* are outdated terms that were used to designate victims who survived initial submersion injuries, but died after 24 hours. Fifteen percent of near drowning victims who are conscious at the time of hospital admission die of complications (Modell 1971). *Postimmersion Syndrome*, a contemporary term that replaces the terms *secondary drowning* and *delayed drowning*, refers to complications that cause a victim to collapse after rescue. Membrane damage to the lungs from either freshwater or saltwater causes noncardiogenic pulmonary edema (acute respiratory distress syndrome), which impairs blood oxygenation (Weinstein and Krieger 1996).

Immersion Syndrome designates a situation in which the victim dies suddenly after entering cold water. The sudden shock of icy water—especially on the face—can cause involuntary gasping and cardiac arrest. Victims of this syndrome may not struggle (Goode, Duffin, and Miller 1975). Sudden death results from cold-induced heart disorders (Keating and Hayward 1981). The victim drowns from loss of consciousness in water, but immersion syndrome was the initiating factor. Alcoholic intoxication, a factor in half of all drownings, predisposes victims to this syndrome. If you ever fall into icy water, cover your face with your hands to minimize the effects of the cold water on your physiology.

Statistics

Nearly 7,000 people drown every year in the United States. Drowning causes more fatalities than fires do. According to the U.S. Lifesaving Association (Evans 1999), drowning is

- the leading cause of death in children 1 to 2 years of age,
- the second leading cause of death in people 5 to 44 years of age, and
- the third leading cause of accidental death in the United States.

Drowning is a major problem everywhere for people of all ages and the greatest single contributor to toddler deaths. Additionally, consider the following:

- 90 percent of drownings occur at unsupervised sites (Smith and Smith 1994).
- Two out of three submersion victims were under the influence of alcohol or drugs (National Institute on Alcohol Abuse and Alcoholism 1981, 83).
- Men are four times more likely than women to die of drowning (U.S. Centers for Disease Control 1985, 30).
- There are no accurate records of the number of submersion victims who eventually die (Smith and Smith 1994, 15).
- The incidence of near drowning has been estimated to be up to 20 times greater than reported drownings (Baker, O'Neill, and Karpf 1984, 155) because many victims do not seek medical help.

The message from these statistics is clear: Drowning is a significant problem that merits much more attention than it receives. The first course of action is prevention; the second is rescue; the third is first aid and evacuation; and the final course of action is medical care. The objective of this book is to provide information about the first three actions.

Causes of Submersion Injuries

Nearly half of all drownings occur to children younger than four years of age. The highest rate is among children one to two years old. The single greatest contributing factor is inadequate supervision. The following statistics from a comprehensive study by the U.S. Consumer Product Safety Commission (1994b) are alarming:

- Most victims were "supervised" by one or both parents.
- 46 percent of victims were last seen in the house.
- 23 percent of victims were last seen in the yard or on the porch or patio.

- 31 percent of victims were in or around a swimming pool before the accident.
- 69 percent of victims were not expected to be at or in the water.
- 75 percent of victims had been missing from sight for five minutes or less.
- Drowning is a silent death. There is no splashing or calling out for help.

Insulating covers for swimming pools have increased swimming pool drownings. The covers can support light toys, but not the weight of a child. When a child steps onto the cover to retrieve a toy, the cover slides away from the edge of the pool, the child falls into the pool, and the cover then slides back over the child. Not only is the child trapped beneath the cover, but he cannot be seen beneath the water. Pool drains can create suction strong enough to cause disembowelment. Special drain covers or dual drains can help prevent entrapment drownings.

The second age group at greatest risk for submersion injuries is teenage males. Males account for 92 percent of the drowning deaths for ages 15 through 19 (Spyker 1985). Both swimmers and nonswimmers are included in this group. Contributing factors include alcohol (used in more than 50 percent of the accidents), excessive loss of body heat, accidental falls, headfirst dives resulting in spinal injury, hyperventilation (excessive breathing) followed by breath holding and blackout, and failure to wear personal flotation devices while boating. Young men tend to take more risks than young women do and may therefore be at greater risk.

Seizure disorders are a too-frequent cause of drowning. A study conducted in Seattle, Washington, found that 80 percent of the bathtub drownings of children over age five were caused by seizures that occurred while the victims were bathing unattended (Quan et al. 1989).

Five-gallon plastic buckets also pose a hazard to toddlers, who have large heads and a high center of gravity. When the child reaches into the bucket, loses balance, and falls inverted into even a couple of inches of water, drowning is likely because she is unable to tip the bucket over to right herself. Over 300 children have drowned in buckets since 1984 (National SAFE Kids Campaign n.d.).

Drowning also poses a risk to hot tub and spa users. Hair and body part entanglements from pump intakes can trap people underwater if not configured correctly. Heat-related illness is a major factor that causes drowning in hot tubs and spas. Temperature-related disasters are addressed in chapter 3.

Some, but not all, scuba diving accidents may cause drowning. On average, one hundred divers die every year while scuba diving. Scuba-related drownings are discussed in chapter 7.

Approximately 17 percent of drownings are related to recreational boating accidents. Chapter 8 addresses boating-related disasters.

Pathophysiology

Pathophysiology is the term for "functional changes associated with or resulting from disease or injury." Those interested in rescue and first aid should understand the functional changes that occur in the human body while drowning.

The drowning process is varied because circumstances vary. The water may be warm or cold. The victim may be young or old, a swimmer or a nonswimmer, insulated or noninsulated, healthy or unhealthy, impaired by drugs or alcohol or unimpaired, injured or uninjured, and so forth. This section describes a general pattern of the drowning process and its effects on body functions.

Drowning commences with a disruption of the breathing pattern, whether the victim is breathing periodically or breath holding. Loss of consciousness, aspiration of water, seizures, injury, hyperventilation, exhaustion, drug use, or other factors may cause the interruption. The broken breathing pattern usually causes panic and struggling, but many victims succumb without any signs of distress. Once a disruption of the breathing pattern occurs, a victim's actions are likely to shift from desirable to instinctive as illustrated in table 1.1.

A good swimmer relaxes muscles not being used, controls breathing, conserves energy, and feels calm. A person in distress in the water is tense, struggles, is filled with anxiety, and gasps. The person in distress breathes a combination of air and water and coughs, which reduces buoyancy by lowering lung volume. Shallow, rapid breathing caused by stress also lowers lung volume and buoyancy. Victims must exert more energy to keep their heads above water. Automatic, instinctive swimming movements ensue unless the victims are incapacitated. When victims are no longer able to raise their heads above the surface to breathe and can no longer hold their breath, they will inhale water. When oxygen levels within the body become too low, loss of consciousness occurs. Whether conscious or unconscious, victims who must breathe will swallow water reflexively in an effort to keep the water from entering their lungs. When the urge to breathe intensifies, swallowing will yield to a deep breath. A spasm of the vocal cords to lock the throat shut and prevent water from invading the lungs is a final reflexive action by the body to protect the lungs. The combination of the

Table 1.1   Desired Versus Instinctive Aquatic Actions

Desired actions	Instinctive actions
Controlled breathing	Uncontrolled breathing
Controlled movements	Uncontrolled movements
Controlled exertion	Maximum exertion
Perceptual awareness	Perceptual narrowing
Controlled emotions	Uncontrolled emotions (panic)

lack of oxygen and the inability to breathe causes unconsciousness, cessation of movement, and sinking. The throat will remain closed until oxygen levels are too low to support muscle action. When the throat relaxes and opens, all protective mechanisms are disabled, and the victim's instinctive breathing movements fill the lungs with water. The heart rate gradually decreases, cardiac arrest ensues, and a final convulsion occurs before death. Figure 1.3 summarizes the sequence of events typical in a drowning.

Pulmonary changes are among the primary effects of the drowning process. The lungs contain a protein substance called surfactant that reduces the surface tension of the microscopic air sacs (alveoli) in the lungs where gas exchange with the bloodstream occurs. Dilution of surfactant by the invasion of freshwater causes the air sacs to collapse and increases the effort required to ventilate the lung. Medical personnel use positive expiratory end pressure (PEEP) devices to maintain some pressure in the lungs during resuscitation to prevent the alveoli from collapsing during each expiration. Water in the air sacs causes fluid and protein to be drawn into the lungs from the blood. Collapsed or water-filled air sacs cause circulation to the sacs to shift to a shunting blood vessel, bypass-

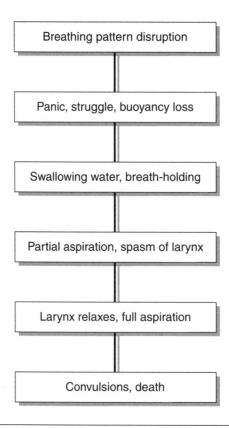

Figure 1.3 Drowning sequence—active victim.

ing the air sac and eliminating gas exchange (see figure 1.4). These problems combine to reduce the amount of oxygen absorbed into the bloodstream and distributed to the body. When oxygen levels become too low, organ damage and death may occur.

Additional pulmonary problems include poisoning from aspirated chemicals in water (e.g., cleaning solution in a five-gallon bucket), aspiration pneumonia from contaminated water or stomach contents, and body core cooling from inspired cold water. Chapter 3 has additional information concerning temperature-related problems.

When heart rates and rhythms alter they become life-threatening changes that affect body function. The heart can be shocked into fatal rhythms when an unprotected victim is thrust suddenly into icy cold water. Stress and cold water may combine to cause fatal heart rhythms for adventurers who have marginal levels of physical fitness. Lack of oxygen can damage the heart and cause cardiac arrest. Chapter 4 discusses cardiac issues in more detail.

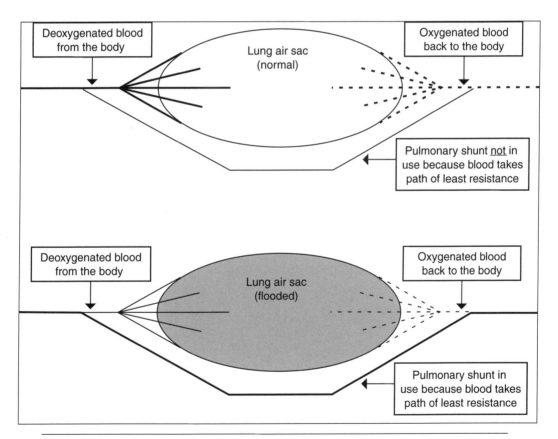

Figure 1.4 Blood normally flows through the capillaries surrounding the alveoli (tiniest air sacs) in the lungs, but submersion injuries can cause circulation to bypass the water-filled air sacs via the shunts.

Blood alterations following submersion injuries affect body function and lead to Postimmersion Syndrome. When oxygen levels are low, cellular function produces acids in the blood. Increased blood acidity can seriously affect the heart, brain, kidneys, liver, and other organs. The severity of metabolic acidosis may be decreased in cold water submersion victims. The metabolic rate of the average person decreases approximately 10 percent for each degree Celsius below 37 degrees (98.6 degrees Fahrenheit) (Gabrielli and Layon 1997). The core temperature of an adult can decrease three degrees in 10 minutes. Cold water also causes blood to be shunted from the body surface and extremities to conserve core heat. As more blood is shifted to the core of the body, the heart must pump a greater volume with each contraction. In such situations the workload of the heart can increase by as much as 30 percent (Seley 1980). The kidneys and other organs must also process more blood. The kidneys will remove fluid from the blood to reduce volume and pressure. Water pressure on the body increases blood pressure. When the victim of a submersion injury is removed from the water, the combined effect of blood acids, decreased blood volume, the sudden drop in blood pressure, and the inability of the cold heart to respond quickly to the decreased pressure can cause the victim to collapse from shock. This syndrome can be fatal and affects rescue procedures, which are described in chapter 2.

The most important factor affecting the recovery from submersion injuries is permanent neurological functional changes caused by lack of oxygen to the brain. Prompt resuscitation of victims using the highest possible concentration of oxygen is critical to survival and recovery without impairment. Resuscitation procedures are explained in detail in chapter 9.

Finally, it is important to keep in mind that many of the physiological problems of submersion injuries can cause complications that can become fatal hours after an accident. It is imperative that all submersion injury victims receive a medical evaluation by a physician at a medical facility. It is not uncommon for victims who revive at the scene to feel embarrassed and refuse medical care. They must be convinced that the situation is serious and that they must have medical attention. If the victim is not examined, the result could be fatal.

Prevention

In terms of drowning, an ounce of prevention is worth far more than a pound of cure. Rescues and first aid are required because prevention has failed. The following recommendations are a summary of recommendations made by the U. S. Consumer Product Safety Commission (1994b); Children's Hospital and Medical Center, Seattle, Washington (1992); the American Trauma Society (2001); the Coast Guard Auxiliary (undated); and the American Academy of Pediatrics (undated).

Prevent children from drowning by doing the following:

1. Have them wear Coast Guard–approved personal flotation devices. Do not depend on swimming ability, flotation toys, or flotation armbands.
2. Surround swimming pools and backyard ponds with fencing (five feet minimum height) that has a latch that is out of reach of small children. Gates should be self-closing and self-latching. Encourage neighbors to take the same precautions.
3. Equip swimming pools with anti-entrapment drain covers and/or dual drains, depth markers, rescue equipment, and alarms with remote receivers. Remove toys in and around a pool when it is not in use.
4. Install alarms on residence doors that lead to swimming pools.
5. Supervise children continuously! Swimming lessons or flotation devices are never a substitute for supervision.
6. Look in the swimming pool first when a child is missing. Seconds count!
7. Discuss pool safety and supervision with baby-sitters.
8. Prohibit reckless swimming and horseplay.
9. Empty five-gallon buckets immediately after use and store them out of children's reach.
10. Have safety latches on toilet seats and keep the seats down and latched when not in use.

Prevent teenage submersion injuries by enforcing the following rules:

1. Wear a Coast Guard–approved personal flotation device when boating or when swimming across a lake or river.
2. Assess possible hazards before entering the water. Never dive into murky water.
3. Avoid alcohol consumption when swimming, diving, or boating.
4. Avoid swimming, jumping, or falling into cold water.
5. Avoid swimming and boating during inclement weather.
6. Avoid swift water and currents.
7. Always swim with a partner or group.
8. Ignore dares to swim to a buoy, raft, or some distant object.
9. Never dive into water when the depth is less than nine feet.
10. Never pretend to drown.

Prevent adult submersion injuries by doing the following:

1. Avoid alcohol when participating in water-related recreational activities.
2. Wear a Coast Guard–approved personal flotation device when boating or when swimming across a lake or river.

3. Equip hot tub and spa pump intakes with anti-entrapment covers and limit the time you spend in hot water.

4. Use caution around grates and drains in hot tubs. Suction of hair can cause submerged entrapment. Equip pools, hot tubs, and spas with clearly labeled emergency cutoff switches that are located within view from the pool or spa (see figure 1.5).

5. Keep any electrical devices far away from bathtubs, hot tubs, and spas.

6. Continuously supervise people with seizure disorders while they bathe.

7. Avoid high-risk situations for nonswimmers and weak swimmers (e.g., small sailboats, canoes, whitewater rafts, and inflatable kayaks).

8. Always swim with a partner or group.

9. Avoid hyperventilation (deep, rapid breathing) before breath-hold swims. Loss of consciousness may occur before the urge to breathe occurs.

10. Receive training for technical aquatic activities such as boating, kayaking, and scuba diving.

Figure 1.5 Swimming pools, hot tubs, and spas should be equipped with clearly labeled emergency cutoff switches that are located within view from the pool, tub, or spa.

Key Points

Drowning is the worst submersion injury, but it can be prevented by training, preparation, equipment, continuous supervision, and other prevention methods. Uninterrupted supervision of toddlers and children, restricted access to residential bodies of water, avoidance of alcohol consumption when in and around water, and the wearing of personal flotation devices are the most important preventive measures.

Chapter 2

Recognition and Response

Drowning is a quiet activity. When people reach the point at which they are struggling for air, breathing takes precedence over speech. Once victims have begun the drowning process, they are unable to call out for help. Splashing and thrashing may not be reliable indicators either. Even nonswimmers learn instantly that lifting their hands and arms above water creates weight that pushes them beneath the surface. During the drowning process, hand movements are primarily beneath the surface of the water. The common perception of how a drowning person behaves is not what actually occurs. Indications of the disaster are subtle. Even trained lifeguards fail to recognize when people are beginning to drown.

Learning Goals   By the end of this chapter, you should be able to:

- Define the terms *rescue* and *panic*.
- List six of eight signs that may indicate that a person in the water is in distress.
- List four of five actions that you should take when assessing a victim in distress.
- List the five areas of preparation recommended for aquatic emergency preparedness.
- List five examples of hazards that would preclude a rescue attempt by a lay rescuer.
- List the four general rescue options in order of preference from the most desirable to the least desirable.
- Describe the steps of a water-based rescue.
- Describe six methods recommended for extricating a victim from the water.

You can learn what to look for and identify actions that will help you to save a life. You must act quickly because the drowning sequence happens quickly. A drowning adult without buoyancy struggles at the surface for only about one minute (figure 2.1). After losing consciousness and sinking, the victim must be recovered within a few minutes to ensure survival. As you will learn later in this book, rescue procedures are much more complicated when a victim sinks out of sight. Your goal is to recognize a person in distress in the water and somehow render assistance—all within 60 seconds.

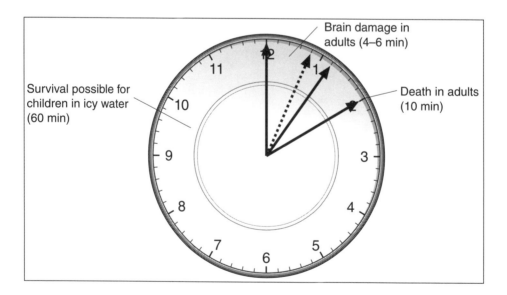

Figure 2.1   The drowning "clock." Adults are not likely to survive suffocation lasting more than 10 minutes, especially in water warmer than 60 degrees Fahrenheit. Children can survive prolonged immersions in cold water (Dueker and Brown 1999).

Recognition

The breathing pattern of a person in the water is a good indicator of the person's condition. Regular, deep breathing is a good sign that the person is not in distress. Reasonable time periods for underwater breath-hold swims are acceptable and not necessarily indicative of distress. Signs of trouble include gasping, coughing, shallow and rapid breathing, and prolonged underwater time (more than two minutes) during breath-hold swims. Since a person can progress from controlled breathing to uncontrolled breathing almost instantly, constant observation is essential for problem recognition. Remember that many drowning victims were unattended for "only a few minutes."

Failure to respond to communications may indicate a problem. If you think that a person may be in distress and you call or signal him and receive no response (especially if he is facing you), be suspicious.

Body position and movement can help you identify potential drowning victims. A conscious person in distress will be low in the water with the head tilted back and the mouth open. An unconscious or incapacitated victim will be motionless and will often be facing downward. The movements of a conscious, distressed person will be jerky. If you can see into or through the water, the victim's hand movements will be outward and downward. Kicking motions will be weak and ineffective. From an underwater view, victims often look as if they are climbing a ladder. Figure 2.2 depicts the "drowning response."

Figure 2.2 The "drowning response." Anyone—strong swimmers included—will resort to instinctive actions when about to drown.

Perceptual narrowing (tunnel vision and "tunnel thinking") will occur as the victim's problems escalate. The victim may not respond to instructions or grasp objects extended or thrown, especially if the victim has to raise a hand above the surface of the water to grab the object. The victim's eyes will appear large and unfocused.

Drownings occur quickly, quietly, and subtly. Potential rescuers need to know what to look for and must oversee an aquatic activity constantly. The formula of "untrained bystanders plus distractions equals drowning" needs to be replaced with "trained observers plus continuous observation equals zero drownings."

Response

Rescue means "to free or save from danger." We will call the act of retrieving a victim from the water a rescue and put first aid for the victim into a different category. The ways to rescue a drowning person are as varied as the circumstances in which people drown. You may only have to lift a child from a few inches of water, or you may need to overcome powerful forces of nature to save a large adult. It is important to know your limitations and to operate within them so that you do not become an additional victim.

Assessment

You should assess any rescue situation for at least a few seconds before taking action. Ideally this would be done because you are overseeing a particular aquatic activity. However, if you happen upon a situation that requires you to take action, pause and size up the predicament and formulate a quick plan of action before reacting. The size-up will help you avoid hazards, identify resources, and act in an organized manner. Examine the area for hazards. Ask bystanders what happened. Look around for possible resources. Determine the fastest possible means for getting to the victim. If possible, delegate responsibilities, such as calling for assistance. The following story emphasizes the critical need for assessment.

IT IS A WARM SUMMER DAY. As you are walking beside the lake, you hear a cry for help from a dock that is only yards away. As you run toward the dock, you see a young woman waving frantically and pointing to a young man who is floating face down in the water. You run onto the dock, jump into the water, grab the young man, and pull him to the dock. Others who have heard the cries for help assist you in pulling the young man from the water. He is unconscious but coughing and breathing. Within minutes emergency medical personnel arrive and the young man regains consciousness. You are elated because you have saved a life. But then you learn that the young man is paralyzed. He had dived headfirst into the shallow water and injured his cervical spine.

You will never know whether you aggravated the damage to his spinal cord by moving his head and neck during the rescue. If you had taken just a few seconds to ask the young woman what had happened, you would have used different rescue techniques (covered later in this chapter), the young man's paralysis may not have been permanent, and you would not be regretting your actions. Remember that assessment comes before action (except in the dictionary).

Preparation

What does preparation entail? In addition to basic rescue equipment, you will need knowledge, skill, the proficiency that comes from practice, and wisdom, which is knowledge and skill rightly applied. Proper preparation also means that you are collected enough to avoid extraordinary risks and to use the best and safest means at your disposal. These principles apply to lay rescuers and professional rescuers alike. Although a citizen may not be trained for water rescues the way a firefighter is trained, both should be able to provide assistance within the scope of their knowledge and skills. A major purpose of this book is to provide both lay and professional responders the knowledge and skills that will help them save victims of submersion injuries.

Prepare yourself by learning rescue techniques. Study the techniques described in this book. Take lifesaving and water rescue courses from organizations listed in appendix A. Become and remain physically fit. Obtain and maintain the rescue and first aid equipment that is listed in various chapters and in appendix B. Practice water rescue skills periodically. I recommend that citizens practice rescue skills at least annually and that professionals practice at least every three months.

You may be thinking, I'm not a professional rescuer. Why do I need all of this preparation? If you spend much time around water, the day may come when you will be called on to perform a rescue. Let's hope that you don't have to look back and wish that you had taken the time and effort to get prepared for a rescue situation before it occurred.

Here's another way to look at this issue: We practice fire drills to save our families from a fire. We have a plan, and we practice the actions periodically. We maintain some limited equipment—fire extinguishers, smoke detectors, and escape ladders. We are not professional firefighters, but in an emergency we can save lives because we are prepared. Water rescue drills for families who engage in aquatic activities should be like fire drills. We should be equipped and practiced, and have a plan.

Hazards

In spite of the best efforts to prepare for an emergency, hazards exist because situations vary greatly. Hazards meriting caution or avoidance include the following:

- Fire
- Potential explosions from watercraft or aircraft
- Vessel or vehicle shift while sinking
- Hazardous materials (e.g., fuel floating on the water)
- Lines, wires, and cables (entanglement)
- Debris
- Entrapment
- Swift water
- Rough water
- Cold water
- Ice
- Downward currents (holes in rivers, dam hydraulics, unusual tidal currents)

Avoid extraordinary risks. If you are unable to save yourself, you will not be able to save someone else. Compounding a problem by creating multiple victims does not help. Learn to distinguish a rescue from a recovery. If the situation is obviously dangerous or the victim has probably expired because of time constraints, wait for a trained and specially equipped recovery team to arrive.

Rescue Options

One action that you need to take during your size-up of the situation is to determine the best way to reach the victim. Always keep in mind that specialized rescues—ice, swift water, or scuba diving—usually require professional rescuers who have special equipment and training. If you are not qualified to undertake a rescue, contact water rescue teams who are prepared for rapid response. Figure 2.3 shows the priority order of rescue response as designated by multiple water rescue technique sources.

Techniques such as "reach" and "throw and tow" may work for a distressed aquatic victim but will not be effective when a person is on the brink of drowning (remember that the person may be experiencing peripheral narrowing).

> The priority of rescue response order is as follows:
>
> 1. Reach
> 2. Throw and tow
> 3. Row
> 4. Go

Figure 2.3 Priority of rescue response.

Because you must physically get to the victim quickly, the rescue techniques that we will focus on are the "row" and "go" procedures. "Row" means the use of watercraft—any watercraft that you are competent to operate. Examples include inflatable boats, kayaks, and personal watercraft. If it floats and you know how to use it, consider using it. "Go" means entering the water yourself and going to the victim in distress. Because it places you in jeopardy, this is the least desirable rescue option.

Reach

The easiest and most desirable form of rescue is to reach out or extend an object to the person in trouble. The person must be fairly close by for this form of rescue. Lie down on a dock and extend a hand. Climb down a ladder into the water and extend a foot. Get a pole or dip net from the pool wall and extend it. Find a tree limb or board and extend it to the victim. Use anything available to increase your reach. When the victim grasps the object that you have extended, retract it slowly so the victim will not lose his grasp.

Throw and Tow

If the victim is too far away to reach with anything, you may be able to use the "throw and tow" rescue technique to provide assistance. Your best option is to throw a rescue bag packed with rope that pays out while you throw it (see figure 2.4). Be sure to throw the rope upstream or up current from the victim

Figure 2.4 Rope bag being thrown to victim. Toss a rescue rope bag upwind, upstream, and beyond the victim using an underhand motion. The inset is a close-up of the throw bag.

so the movement of air or water will move the rope toward the victim and not away from her. Also, throw the end of the rope beyond the victim. If your throw is short, you will have to retrieve the line and attempt another throw. If you must retrieve the line for another attempt, simply coil it on the ground instead of packing it back into the bag. Scoop some water into the bag to give it weight and toss it quickly before the water leaks from the bag. Throw the rope underhanded as though you were tossing a horseshoe. Once the victim has the rope, ask her to wrap it around her body or arm so it will not slip from her grasp when you pull her gently to safety.

An inner tube or a life ring on the end of a line is a good throwing device. Toss the ring in a manner somewhere between an underhand toss and a sidearm toss while keeping your arm straight (see figure 2.5). Practice will be required to determine the release point. Remember to toss the tube or ring up current, upwind, and beyond the victim. When the victim has the ring, ask him to place it around his body so the float will not slip from his grasp when you pull him to safety.

Figure 2.5 When throwing a rescue ring, an underhand motion is more accurate than a sidearm motion.

Fire departments can extend a fire hose that is capped on the ends and inflated with air. The hose may be a single line, or it may be a double line tied in the middle to form a loop. A single hose is "steered" by twisting it in the water. A double line may be steered by pushing and pulling on the two lines. Fifty feet of 2.5-inch hose will support eight adults in the water and is an extremely valuable tool when there are multiple victims and there is enough time to deploy an engine and the air-filled hoses (see figure 2.6).

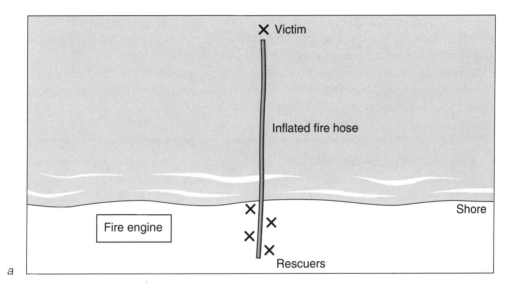

a

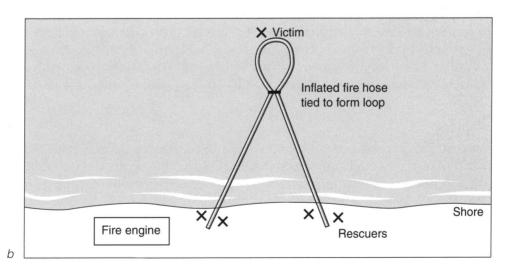

b

Figure 2.6 *(a)* A single inflated fire hose can be steered to a victim by twisting the hose. *(b)* When there is sufficient hose and time available, a double hose with a loop in the end can be steered more easily than a single hose.

If you do not have a rope to throw to a person in distress, throw the person anything that will provide flotation. This can be a difficult task because many flotation objects are difficult to throw accurately or far because of their shape. Choose objects that will be easy for the victim to hold onto. Advance preparation helps greatly.

Row

Whenever possible, use some type of watercraft (that you are capable of operating safely) to reach a victim who is drowning. The time that it takes you to get the vessel into operation will be more than made up for by the speed with which you can reach the victim. You will have a platform of safety from which to work, and the platform also can be used for first aid procedures, such as CPR.

Remember the rules of water rescue. Survey the situation, use the best means at your disposal, use a watercraft whenever possible, and avoid exposing yourself to risks for which you are not equipped.

I AM A VOLUNTEER FIREFIGHTER. Although we do not have a boat, our fire station responds to marine rescue emergency calls. Usually we serve as spotters and provide medical assistance. One evening we responded to a call about a man hanging onto the side of a boat and calling for help. Our unit arrived on the scene first and observed the man about 100 yards offshore. He said that he had the rope to a crab trap around his leg and that he could not let go of the boat or the trap would pull him underwater. He asked us to hurry because he could not hang on much longer. Lacking a vessel and equipment that would allow us to enter into and move through the cold water, we surveyed the situation. Several small dinghies were chained to posts along the shore. We took bolt cutters from our truck, cut a chain, commandeered a dinghy, rowed to the victim, and rescued him. He said that he would not have been able to hold on much longer. A rescue boat did not arrive until after we had rescued the man. A tragedy was averted.

Go

This section presents general information and techniques pertaining to the rescue of swimmers and nonswimmers who are struggling at the surface of the water. For more information about specific water emergencies, see chapter 6 (swimming), chapter 7 (scuba diving), and chapter 8 (watercraft). Do not attempt these techniques without training, practice, and equipment!

Before attempting a water-based rescue, all other forms of rescue must first be ruled out. A water-based rescue should be your last resort and should be attempted only if you are confident that your safety will not be jeopardized unnecessarily.

Rule 1: Use the fastest and most direct route to get to a distressed swimmer.

I WAS A VISITING DIGNITARY for a scuba diving instructor workshop in Northern California. We were conducting in-water exercises behind a breakwater that extended well into a bay. A strong current ran along the end of the breakwater. Several divers surfaced at the end of the breakwater and fought the current at the surface attempting to get back into the sheltered area. One of the divers became exhausted, dropped his weight belt, and called for help. The workshop director and two staff members heard the cry and sprang into action. One staff member ran into the water, donned his swim fins, and began swimming toward the end of the breakwater. A second staff member walked and climbed along the large rocks of the breakwater, making his way to the end. What I witnessed was impressive. Although the second rescuer had to make his way from rock to rock along the entire length of the breakwater, he was able to assist the diver out of the water before the swimming rescuer was even halfway to the scene! Use the fastest route.

After a day of teaching advanced techniques to a group of divers from the U.S. Bureau of Reclamation, several of the divers and I were relaxing on the balcony of a motel. Across the road, about 75 yards away, was a swimming pool surrounded by an eight-foot-tall chain-link fence. A young woman was reading a book in a chaise lounge at the shallow end of the pool. Several children were playing in the shallow end of the pool, and several older children and adults were swimming in the deep end. Suddenly one of the divers in our group leaped to his feet, exclaimed "that kid is drowning," and jumped from the second-story balcony to the ground. He ran across the road, climbed the chain-link fence, leaped to the pool deck, and pulled a sputtering three-year-old girl from the shallow end of the pool. The woman in the chaise lounge rushed to the girl. The rescuer and the mother had a discussion. When the rescuer returned he said that he had told the woman, who was the girl's mother, to watch her more closely because the girl had nearly drowned right under her nose. I was impressed that the rescuer had gone to the distressed little girl in a straight line, right over the balcony, instead of taking the stairs.

Rule 2: Have and use flotation.

As a rescuer, you need flotation for yourself and for the victim. Professional rescuers always wear personal flotation devices (PFDs) (see figure 2.7). Lay rescuers should emulate professionals. Remember that your personal safety comes first. If a panicked, struggling victim is able to grasp you and climb on you in an effort to get out of the water, buoyancy can help you survive. Carrying something that floats can be useful to extend to a victim, but the float may not help you. Get in the habit of wearing a PFD when you are around the water (more on this subject later). If you are on shore and may need to effect a rescue, keep a PFD handy so you can don it quickly while sizing up the situation.

The primary reason for using flotation is to support a panicked swimmer. Panic is defined as a sudden, unreasoning, inappropriate, fearful reaction to a real or imagined danger. Most people panic when they are drowning. Panicked people are convinced that death is imminent. The best possible way to help a drowning individual overcome panic is to help her regain breathing control (see figures 2.8 and 2.9). You cannot help a victim regain breathing control as long as she is struggling, and you cannot get a panicked person to stop struggling until she is able to keep her head above water and get air. Your job is to provide reassurance and instructions to reduce the victim's physical activity and to encourage breath control. As the victim slowly regains control of her breathing, her peripheral awareness will increase and you will begin to assume control of the situation.

Figure 2.7 Personal flotation devices. The most important factors in the selection of a personal flotation device are proper size and fit.

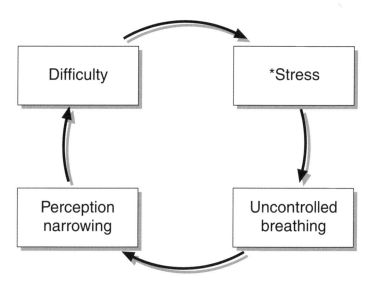

Figure 2.8 The panic cycle.

*Until stress becomes panic

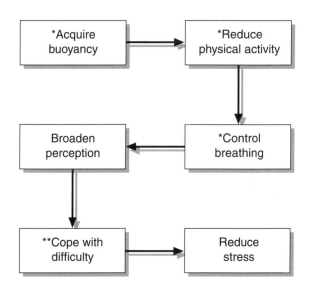

Figure 2.9 Breaking the panic cycle.

*With assistance

**May need assistance

Rule 3: Have rescue equipment, keep it handy, and know how to use it.

Flotation is essential. Swim fins are essential for deep-water rescues. Aquatic rescue breathing techniques are presented later in this book. I recommend the use of a rescue breathing mask, and I always carry one with me when I go scuba diving. After using the mask for a rescue, a friend who witnessed the event asked me, "Where did you get that breathing mask? I have never seen it before." I told him that I always carry it in the pocket of my buoyancy jacket just in case. He then decided to take a scuba rescue class and get a mask.

Trained citizen rescuers do not need elaborate equipment, but they should be prepared. I recommend that they have—as a minimum—swim fins, a personal flotation device, a rescue float with attached line, and a rescue breathing mask (see figure 2.10). An exposure suit also is essential if the water is cold.

Figure 2.10 Minimum rescue equipment for citizens should include fins, personal flotation, a rescue float, an exposure suit (for cold water), and a rescue breathing mask.

Professional rescuers need to be prepared for all contingencies. Each rescuer needs a protective suit, gloves, thermal boots, helmet, swim fins and mask, knife, wire-cutting tool, harness with tether line, personal flotation device, rescue buoy, and rescue breathing mask (see figure 2.11). The rescue team needs rescue lines and floats, an immobilization device, compasses and charts, accountability tags, communications equipment, and more. The team may need a watercraft, a global positioning system for searches, lift bags to secure wreckage, and many other items depending on the type of rescue. Underwater rescues, swift water rescues, ice rescues, and contaminated water rescues—just to name a few situations—require highly specialized rescue equipment.

Figure 2.11 Minimum rescue equipment for a professional rescuer includes an exposure suit, personal flotation, a rescue float, a helmet, mask or goggles, fins, knife, cutters, harness, tether, rescue breathing mask, light, strobe, and signaling devices.

Having rescue equipment is of little value if the user cannot access it quickly and use it effectively. Rescue equipment must be at the ready, and the user must practice using it periodically to maintain proficiency. Both citizens and professionals should schedule regular rescue drills to be prepared for actual emergencies.

Deep-Water Rescue Entries

When you decide that a water-based rescue is the best method to use, delegate responsibilities while you don your rescue equipment. Ask a bystander to call for assistance, and ask another to watch the victim continuously and guide you to the person. If additional people are available, ask one to get the first aid equipment. Keep your eyes on the victim while you assign various tasks.

Watch the victim continuously. If you must enter deep water, place the rescue float horizontal beneath your arms so it will support you when you jump into the water (see figure 2.12). Even if you are wearing a flotation device, your

Figure 2.12 Placing the rescue float level and beneath your arms while entering the water will help keep your head above water to maintain visual contact with the victim.

Figure 2.13 Entering with arms and legs extended and then pulling the legs together and the arms to the sides will also help keep your head above water during a rescue entry.

momentum may cause your head to submerge, so place one leg forward and one leg backward and extend your arms out to the sides as you jump into the water. As soon as you hit the water, pull your legs together quickly and pull your arms to your sides (see figure 2.13). With practice, you should be able to keep your head above water during a deep-water entry.

Rescue Swimming and Approaching

Watch the victim continuously while you swim toward him. Because holding your head above water and swimming for any distance is difficult, swim fins and personal flotation are highly desirable. Pace yourself during the swim. If you swim all out to reach the victim, you can consume more oxygen than you breathe because oxygen stored in your tissues will be depleted. Just about the time that you need energy to assist the victim, you could be out of breath. When your circulation adjusts to the activity, which takes some time, you will catch your "second wind" and be able to sustain the activity.

When you approach a victim in distress at the surface, attempt to make eye contact and establish verbal communications. If the victim can talk to you, the situation has not yet reached the critical stage and you may be able to get the person to help himself. Provide reassurance, even if the person does not respond when you speak to him.

Unless the victim's head is beneath the water, stop a few feet from the person and extend flotation by pushing it beneath the surface and under the victim's extended arms. Panicked persons may not reach above the water to grasp a float, but they will instinctively grasp it when they feel its support from beneath.

If the victim is not able to keep his head above water, you must make contact and provide support immediately. If the person loses consciousness and sinks, the rescue will be much more difficult, if not impossible. Techniques for underwater rescues are presented in chapter seven. Grasp the top of the victim's opposite wrist with one hand, pull him toward you, and turn the front of his body so it is not facing you (see figure 2.14). Use your opposite

Figure 2.14 To provide immediate support while protecting yourself, grasp the victim's opposite wrist, pull and turn the victim, and provide support beneath the arm. Complete the maneuver by pulling the victim's arm downward and moving yourself behind the victim's shoulder.

hand to lift the victim upward and provide support. The need for personal flotation during rescues is obvious because you may need to support two people. Attempting a water-based rescue without flotation could cause your death. Don't ever take that chance.

If a panicked victim is able to grasp you, your escape route is downward, which is the last place the victim wants to go. Tuck your chin and push upward on the victim's arms at the elbows. As you sink beneath the surface, the victim will release you. Push away from the person, surface, and try again. Remember to grasp the opposite wrist and turn the victim so he will not be facing you when you make contact.

Assisting

When you have established buoyancy for a panicked victim, your next task is to help the person regain control of breathing. Tell the person to stop moving, rest, and breathe. Avoid yelling. Use a calm, firm, reassuring voice. Once the victim's breathing is controlled, conversation will be possible. Find out what happened and decide the best way to assist the victim from the water. Many times all that will be necessary is for you to accompany the victim while she swims to safety. At other times you may have to transport the victim using a tired swimmer's carry (see figure 2.15) or a bicep push (see figure 2.16). I prefer to push a victim instead of towing whenever possible because pushes allow eye contact, monitoring, and better communication.

Figure 2.15 Use a tired swimmer's carry to assist an exhausted swimmer.

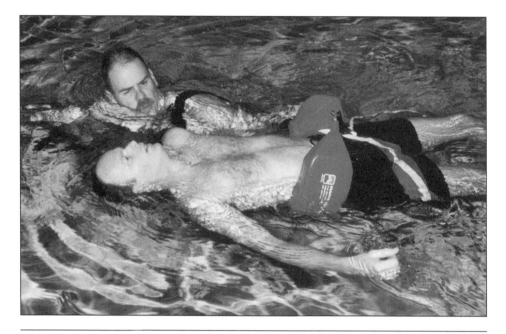

Figure 2.16   The bicep push allows a rescuer to monitor and reassure a victim.

If the person in distress has a cramp, provide buoyancy and help release the cramp by gently stretching the cramped muscle. Avoid pounding or massaging the muscle. Calf muscles cramp most frequently. To release a cramped calf muscle, provide buoyancy, extend the person's leg, and push the toe end of the foot toward the knee, stretching the muscle on the back of the leg as shown in figure 2.17.

When the victim is unconscious, your task is obviously more difficult. Position the victim face up at the surface and place a float under his back to support him (see figure 2.18). Assess the mouth and throat. If you see anything in the mouth, turn the victim's head to the side and sweep the material clear. When the airway is clear, look, listen, and feel for breathing for five seconds. If the victim is not breathing, evaluate the situation. If you can get the victim to shore or a platform within a few seconds, do so. If shore or a platform is distant and you know how to do aquatic rescue breathing, provide ventilations while you tow the victim to safety. Do not bother with assessment of circulation because CPR is not effective in the water. Rescue breathing while towing a victim is a strenuous activity, even while wearing swim fins. It is extremely important for a rescuer to have and use rescue equipment.

Rescue Exits

Getting a victim out of the water is one of the most difficult tasks of a rescue. You will be tired from your efforts, the victim will be slippery and heavy, and

Figure 2.17 The key to releasing a cramp is stretching the cramped muscle.

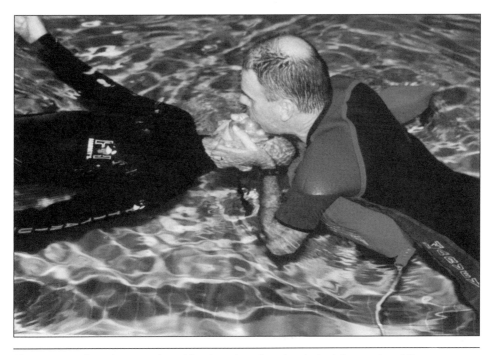

Figure 2.18 Aquatic rescue breathing is easier when the victim is buoyant and the rescuer can use the rescue float for support.

the circumstances can be difficult. Obtain help if at all possible. Many people will simply stand and watch a rescue. If you ask people for help, most will lend a hand. If you don't ask, they often assume that you do not need it. Use caution to avoid injuring yourself. Strained muscles, especially back injuries, may occur if you do not have assistance.

Consider possible neck and spinal injuries. If there are indications of a spinal cord injury and the victim is in warm water and breathing, float the victim face up in the water and keep the head, neck, and back in as straight an alignment as possible. Wait for professional help to arrive with immobilization equipment. If the victim is not breathing and you can get people to help support the victim in the water, use a rescue breathing mask and a jaw-thrust maneuver to do rescue breathing in the water until professional help arrives. When you are alone and the situation is critical, the water is deep, and especially when the water is cold, you will have to risk the victim's permanent disability to save the person's life. Do not delay extrication. Quickly remove the victim from the water using the best possible means to minimize movement of the head, neck, and spine.

Chapter 3 addresses problems related to cold water. If the water temperature is less than 70 degrees Fahrenheit and the victim has been immersed for more than five minutes, it is important to keep the victim as horizontal as possible during a rescue exit. Pulling a victim from the water suddenly in a vertical position may cause circulatory collapse. Allowing a conscious victim to climb from the water can have the same consequence. The reasons for this are explained in chapter 3. If a victim is unconscious and not breathing, use any means necessary to extricate her from the water to initiate first aid promptly. But do try to use one of the following techniques to keep a victim horizontal whenever possible:

1. When help is available and the bottom is shallow and sloping, get bystanders to help, and use a hammock carry.

2. When help is not available and the bottom is shallow and sloping, float the victim to shallow water, place the float line or a rescue strap under the victim's arms, and drag the person to dry land.

3. When help is available and the water is deep, get bystanders to help and use loops of line under the victim's arms and legs to lift the victim.

4. Attach netting or construction fence to a boat or dock to form a device that quickly rolls a victim out of the water (see figure 2.19).

5. If a ladder is readily available, it makes an excellent device for lifting and carrying a victim out of the water (see figure 2.20).

A loop formed from one-inch nylon webbing, similar to a firefighter's hose strap, is a useful tool for water rescues. It is compact and has multiple uses. The circumference of the loop is about 10 feet. A line attached to a

Figure 2.19 Parbuckling is a lifting technique that keeps a victim horizontal and uses pulley mechanics to halve the victim's weight.

Figure 2.20 A ladder lift and carry is effective when a ladder is available. The Germans used this technique successfully for water rescues during World War I.

Figure 2.21   A rescue strap is useful for several rescue exit situations.

rescue float is an alternative, but a strap is less painful for a victim than a line (see figure 2.21).

When the water is warm, the immersion time is brief, or the situation is time-critical, consider using one of the following extrication methods:

1. Place a line or rescue strap under the victim's arms and around the chest and pull the person from the water (see figure 2.21). This method is better than bending over and grasping the victim's armpits, which could cause an injury to your back. Always try to get help to divide the weight of the victim.

2. When the distance to the water is small, face the victim toward the platform, place his hands on the edge, and hold them there while you climb out of the water. Pull the victim halfway onto the platform, fold him at the waist, and then grab one of his legs and roll him onto the platform (see figure 2.22, *a-d*).

a

b

c

d

Figure 2.22 *(a)* Step 1: Place your arms beneath the victim's arms and lift him onto the exit surface. *(b)* Step 2: Move to the victim's side and pin his hands with your hand. *(c)* Step 3: Exit the water, grasp the victim's wrists, and lift the victim. *(d)* Step 4: Fold the victim to the deck at the waist and rotate him onto the deck by pulling on his legs.

Figure 2.23 When using the ladder carry, lean back as far as possible and always lift the leg supporting the victim first.

3. Although difficult and requiring practice, a victim can be carried up a ladder by a fit rescuer, who must keep the knee supporting the victim higher than the groin to avoid having the victim slip from the leg (see figure 2.23).

Key Points

Early recognition of a victim who is about to drown is critical. Rescue techniques should pose minimal jeopardy for the rescuer, and water-based rescue attempts should be the last resort. Good first aid procedures are vital. Training in CPR and first aid should be current.

Part II

Physiological Considerations

Chapter 3

Water and Body Temperature Considerations

Water is a fantastic compound with amazing properties. Still water conducts heat 25 times faster than air. Moving water has an effect similar to wind chill in air. Water moving at a speed of five knots causes a tenfold increase in body heat loss. A human body in this situation would lose 250 times more heat to the water than to still air at the same temperature! Figure 3.1 summarizes the properties of water, which is just as amazing with heat as it is with cold—the absence of heat. Raising the temperature of equal weights of air and water one degree Celsius requires four times more heat for the water. Because water is 800 times denser than air, raising the temperature of equal *volumes* of air and water requires 3,200 times more heat for the water!

IN APRIL 2000, A 16-YEAR-OLD FEMALE from Washington State was a passenger in a canoe when the vessel capsized on the cold, swift-flowing Wenatchee River. The water wrapped the aluminum boat around a bridge pillar, trapping the young woman between the vessel and the pillar. Two other occupants of the boat were thrown overboard and managed to swim to shore. Bystanders could do little as they watched the teenager's arm reach out from beneath the canoe and wave for help. The hand went limp after a few minutes. A sheriff's boat reached the scene quickly after a call to 911, but the rescuer was unable to free the trapped victim. A second rescue vessel arrived, but those rescuers were also unsuccessful. Finally, a fire engine arrived on the bridge. One boat rammed the canoe while a cable from the fire truck above pulled on the vessel. The canoe eventually was dislodged from the pillar and the young woman was freed, but she had been trapped underwater for at least 45 minutes. Ambulance crew members initiated CPR and transported the young woman to a local hospital where doctors were able to restart her heart. The teenager's body temperature had dropped to 77 degrees Fahrenheit in the water, which was in the low 40s. The 16-year-old remained in critical condition for days, but eventually made a remarkable recovery. Her mental status is normal. Rehabilitation has helped her regain near-normal motor functions. She is a living, walking miracle.

Learning Goals *By the end of this chapter, you should be able to:*

▶ Explain why the properties of water cause body heat loss faster than air and why water has a great capacity to absorb heat.

▶ Explain why children and elderly people can survive prolonged immersions in cold water.

▶ List three factors that affect an individual's ability to survive a prolonged immersion.

▶ Define hypothermia and hyperthermia.

▶ List at least five predisposing factors for hypothermia.

▶ Explain how to minimize the risk of involuntarily gasping water if you fall into cold water.

▶ Explain why good swimmers become incapacitated rapidly in cold water.

▶ Explain why a victim is likely to experience circulatory collapse if pulled vertically from cold water.

▶ List two potential physiological hazards that may result from entering cold water without adequate insulation.

▶ Differentiate between mild and severe hypothermia.

▶ Explain why victims rescued from cold water must be handled gently.

▶ Describe basic first aid procedures for hypothermia.

- List five recommendations to minimize the effects of hypothermia on a person who is suddenly immersed in cold water without adequate insulation.
- Differentiate between heat exhaustion and heat stroke.
- List five signs and symptoms of hyperthermia.
- Describe basic first aid procedures for hyperthermia.

Density

Air = 0.08*
Water = 62–64*
Effect = 800 times greater

Thermal conduction

Air = 0.17
Water = 3.86–4.12
Effect = 22–24 times greater

Heat capacity

Air = 0.24
Water = 0.94–1.0
Effect = 3.9–4.1 times greater

Figure 3.1 Water properties compared to air.
*Pounds per cubic foot.

Water's thermal properties also can cause overheating problems when the water is hot. Fatalities in hot tubs and hot springs frequently are related to the effects of elevated body temperature. Rescuers must understand the effects of temperature on the immersed human body because they affect rescue and first aid procedures.

The good news is that people—like the teenager in the opening story—can survive prolonged submersions (greater than 15 minutes) in cold water. The record is a two-and-a-half-year-old Salt Lake City girl who recovered completely after 66 minutes of submersion in water that was 41 degrees Fahrenheit! Children cool quickly because their heads are large in proportion to their bodies, their skin is thin, and they have a small mass (see figure 3.2). Elderly victims also cool quickly because their skin is thin, their circulation is decreased, and their metabolic rate is slower. Scientists speculate as to why the cooling increases the

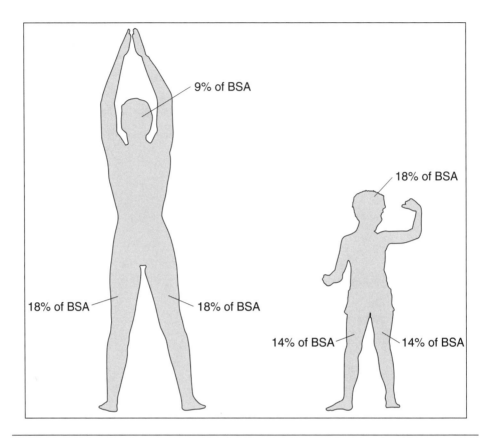

9% of BSA

18% of BSA

18% of BSA

18% of BSA

14% of BSA

14% of BSA

Figure 3.2 A comparison of the body surface area (BSA) of adults versus children and infants. Note that the head (high heat loss area) of the child is proportionally larger than that of an adult, and the legs (low heat loss area) are smaller.

survival time from a normal range of 10 minutes without breathing, but there is no question that victims can survive longer submersions when retrieved from cold water.

IN FEBRUARY 1995, A 61-YEAR-OLD WOMAN pulled her car up to the shore of Lake Washington in Seattle to rest for a few moments. She awoke in a hospital staring up into the faces of nurses and doctors. She could not recall how her car ended up in the lake. Police said that the ignition was turned on and the transmission was in gear when her car entered the water. Bystanders called the fire department to recover a car that had gone into the water. A firefighter investigating the car saw the woman's legs through the windshield. The woman was submerged for 15 minutes in water that was 36 degrees Fahrenheit. She lived, but she did not recover completely. The elderly woman is legally blind, has lost her peripheral vision, and has short-term memory impairment.

ON MARCH 6, 1996, A 62-YEAR-OLD HEALTHY MALE construction worker was operating a tractor on the ice at a bridge construction site on the Red River in Winnipeg, Canada. The tractor broke through the ice and went into water that was 36 to 37 degrees Fahrenheit. The victim was submerged for 15 minutes until a crane was able to hook the tractor and raise it with the worker strapped into his seat. An additional 3 minutes were required to extricate the victim from the tractor and transport him up the riverbank to medical personnel. Miraculously, the man survived. He has persistent memory difficulties and minor neurological abnormalities.

The bad news is that not everyone survives prolonged submersion, even when the water is cold. In a study of documented cases of prolonged submersions in icy water, 75 percent of the victims were children (Orlowski 1988). Factors that decrease an adult's chances of survival in similar conditions include struggle or panic (which release chemicals that are detrimental), water that is warmer than 50 degrees Fahrenheit, or heart rhythm abnormalities that may be caused by sudden immersion into cold water (see chapter 4).

Hypothermia

Hypothermia is a term describing a body core temperature that is below normal (see figure 3.3). The condition may be localized (frostbite) or generalized, mild

Photo courtesy of John Kessler

Figure 3.3 Specialty equipment and training are required in extremely cold water to avoid hypothermia.

- Immersion
- Activity level
- Water movement (current, chop)
- Water and air temperatures
- Physical structure
- Insulation (natural or man-made)
- Wet clothing
- Weather conditions
- Age extremes
- Medical conditions
- Medications
- Drugs (especially alcohol)
- Tobacco use
- Emotional stress
- Injuries

Figure 3.4 Hypothermia risk factors.

The practical risk of hypothermia begins in water colder than 75 degrees Fahrenheit and can occur after extended periods in water warmer than 85 degrees Fahrenheit.

or severe. Mortality from severe generalized body cooling is high because the victims are prone to ventricular fibrillation (a fatal heart rhythm). Onset of hypothermia may be sudden or gradual. The ability of the body to regulate its temperature is lost when the core temperature reaches 95 degrees Fahrenheit. Victims become comatose when the body's core temperature drops to about 79 degrees Fahrenheit. Some victims have survived with core temperatures as low as 64 degrees Fahrenheit (Mistovich et al. 2000). The medical rule for hypothermic victims is that patients are not dead until they are warm and dead. Do not abandon resuscitative efforts because a person appears dead. That victim may live when rewarmed and resuscitated at a medical facility. For that reason, first aid should be rendered to hypothermic submersion victims. A list of predisposing risk factors for body heat loss is presented in figure 3.4.

Physiology

DURING THE WINTER IN THE 1970s, a young California man bet his friends that he could dive through a hole in the ice in a mountain lake, swim 50 feet underwater, and surface through another hole cut through the ice. Wearing only a swimming suit, the man dived into the frigid water. When he did not surface, his friends summoned rescue personnel. The victim was found only a few feet from the point at which he entered the water. His lack of knowledge about cold water physiology caused his death.

Body heat is a function of *heat loss* versus *heat production* (see figure 3.5). The initial body response to immersion cooling is to increase the metabolic rate to elevate heat production. Decreasing core temperature from immersion heat loss quickly decreases metabolism. The cooling rate of the body in cold water is nearly linear when the core begins to cool. You cannot produce enough heat to offset the tremendous thermal properties of water.

The water temperature does not have to be low to cause hypothermia. Extended immersion in water that can be tolerated initially can still lead to hypothermia. Every minute that an unprotected person spends in water is equal to one hour in air at the same temperature. The colder the water is, the more likely a person immersed in it will be to drown, regardless of swimming ability.

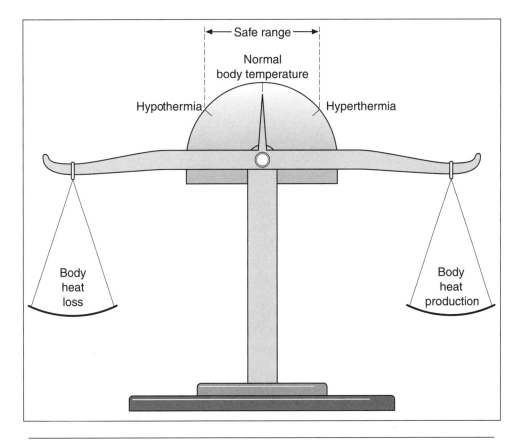

Figure 3.5 Excessive heat loss or heat retention can cause thermal imbalance in the human body.

Table 3.1 Body Systems Deteriorating From Hypothermia

Core temperature (degrees Fahrenheit)	Physical effect
97	Increased metabolism, breathing, and heart rate
96	Shivering, poor muscle coordination
95	Maximum shivering, slurred speech
93	Maximum blood pressure, numbness
90	Shivering stops
	Confusion, disorientation, amnesia begin
	Muscle rigidity begins
88	Blood pressure drops
86	Muscles rigid, loss of consciousness, pupils dilate
85	Pulse and breathing rates slow
84	Heart rhythm irregularities may occur
81	Victim appears dead, pupils fixed and dilated
77	Heart rhythm irregularities likely to occur
75	Fluid accumulates in the lungs
72	Heart rhythm irregularities at maximum risk
71	Cardiac arrest likely

Table 3.1 shows the progressive deterioration of body systems as core body temperature decreases during hypothermia.

Breathing

Immediately upon entering water colder than 50 degrees Fahrenheit, a person gasps involuntarily because the diaphragm contracts. If the person is submerged, water will be drawn into the airway. Two actions that may be taken to prevent aspiration when falling into cold water are covering the mouth and nose while falling or turning the body and landing on the back to reduce facial contact with the water as shown in figure 3.6.

Breathing rate and depth may increase up to five times in cold water as the body attempts to increase oxygen uptake to fuel an internal temperature increase. Aspiration of even a small amount of water at this time can trigger the drowning response.

Most people can hold their breath for one minute at room temperature when they are at rest. But people who are submerged without protection and exercising in water colder than 50 degrees Fahrenheit are unable to hold their breath for more than 10 seconds because of the greatly increased metabolic rate as the body attempts to produce heat. Victims trapped beneath overturned boats in cold water are at great risk because of this reduction in breath-hold ability.

Figure 3.6 Protecting facial nerves from sudden contact with cold water during an unexpected entry can prevent involuntary gasping and water aspiration.

Muscle Use

AFTER A MEMBER HAD FALLEN OVERBOARD DURING A RACE, a local yacht club asked me to give a presentation at the club about hypothermia. The man who had fallen overboard told his story during the presentation. He explained that he was a good swimmer and was in the water only 10 minutes, but that he nearly drowned because he could not move his legs and he was not wearing a personal flotation device.

If a person survives an initial plunge into water colder than 50 degrees Fahrenheit, other life-threatening problems can develop within 10 minutes. Muscles lose strength and coordination and become rigid because the body shunts blood from the extremities in an attempt to reduce heat loss. Even the best swimmer loses the ability to swim as hypothermia progresses. Without flotation, even the best swimmer can drown in very cold water.

OUR FIRE DISTRICT RECEIVED A CALL IN 1999 to assist two kayakers who had capsized at dusk when the wind suddenly increased in Port Susan Bay at Camano Island, Washington. My aid unit was summoned to a residence while marine rescue vessels from other fire stations proceeded to boat launching ramps south of the area where the accident occurred. The reporting party had a telescope pointed at the kayakers, who could be seen through the device for about 10 minutes. Rescue craft crew members began searching for the victims, but were unable to locate them as darkness descended. I phoned the Coast Guard and requested a helicopter. The military rescue craft is equipped with night vision goggles and heat-sensing equipment. The helicopter crew flew a search pattern over the area, but was unable to locate the two victims until they contacted me by radio and I was able to direct them to the last known point using the telescope as a reference. By flying along the course indicated by the telescope, the helicopter crew located the kayakers within a few minutes. I could hear the radio traffic and see the helicopter hovering over the water in the distance. The helicopter hovered for much longer than it should to retrieve the victims. The pilot requested that we establish a landing zone on the island and have a medic unit stand by to receive the two victims because the helicopter did not have any medical personnel or specialized medical equipment aboard.

My aid unit proceeded to the landing zone and arrived there just as the medical personnel were unloading the patients. I was able to talk to the Coast Guard rescue swimmer and asked him why the helicopter had hovered so long. His response was fascinating. The helicopter uses a small basket to retrieve people from the water. The basket is good because the victim is in a position that is nearly horizontal (more on this later in this chapter). The problem that the rescue swimmer had was that the victim's legs were so cold they would not bend! These are dramatic examples of the effect of cold on muscles. Both kayakers were wearing personal flotation devices, survived the ordeal, and recovered completely.

Blood Pressure

A cold, immersed body shunts blood from the extremities to reduce heat loss. In addition, water pressure on the body causes blood to shift into the torso. The increased blood volume in the core of the body increases the volume of blood that passes through the kidneys, which then expel some of the blood as water to reduce the excess volume. Rib bones have high thermal conductivity, so the heart begins to cool during prolonged immersion. When a cold victim is pulled from the water, blood pressure drops rapidly because the external water pressure is removed suddenly. Ordinarily the heart would react quickly with increased output to correct the pressure drop, but a cold heart cannot respond quickly enough to compensate for the rapid drop in blood pressure. Hypovolemic (fluid loss) and cardiogenic (heart-related) shock and circulatory collapse (ultimately cardiac arrest) can result. The combination of these effects is the rationale for extricating victims in a horizontal position (Golden, Hervey, and

Tipton 1991). The drop in blood pressure is much less for a horizontal victim than for a vertical victim.

As body blood cools, the ability of the red blood cells to transport oxygen decreases. Cellular oxygenation throughout the body becomes insufficient. The body produces acids that irritate the heart, cause the brain to swell, and further impair the ability of the body to use oxygen. Metabolic acidosis can be seen in up to 70 percent of near drowning victims (Modell 1976). Toxins released within the body obstruct the smallest vessels that deliver oxygen and further impair oxygen delivery. A vicious cycle begins that can lead to multiple organ failure and death.

Seizures

Sudden immersion into cold water can trigger seizures in people with seizure disorders. A seizure while submerged can be fatal. The sudden shock of cold water immersion also can cause several life-threatening heart conditions, which are explained in chapter 4. Sudden entries into very cold water are a serious matter. Individuals with medical histories that place them at risk need to exercise caution. Epilepsy has been associated with a four- to fivefold increased risk of drowning and near drowning (Orlowski 1982). Good precautions include boating on cold water only in large, stable vessels; wearing insulating clothing; and wearing a personal flotation device at all times when in or around the water.

Vertigo

When a person falls or dives into water colder than 50 degrees Fahrenheit and water enters one ear canal only, a temperature imbalance between the inner ears can cause vertigo. The person may become disoriented and not know which way is up, especially if the water is turbid or the person is under the influence of drugs or alcohol. Panicked victims may actually swim away from the surface.

Recognition

There are several keys to identifying the degree of hypothermia. Citizens without equipment should look for shivering and mental status first. If the person is alert, oriented, and shivering, hypothermia is mild; the body core temperature will be between 90 and 95 degrees Fahrenheit. If the victim has a cold abdomen, is conscious but disoriented, has stiff muscles, and is not shivering, hypothermia is moderate; the body core temperature will be between 91 and 94 degrees Fahrenheit. A cold, unconscious victim who is not shivering is suffering from severe hypothermia; the body core temperature will be below 90 degrees Fahrenheit. Although the victim may appear dead, do not abandon efforts to save the person, who may still be alive.

Professional rescuers should measure the core temperature of hypothermic victims who are not shivering. A special hypothermic thermometer is required because a normal thermometer lacks a scale with temperatures that are low

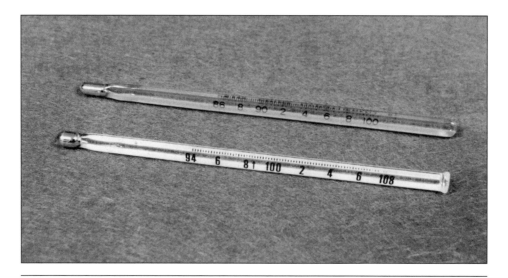

Figure 3.7 A hypothermic thermometer (top) has a lower temperature scale than a standard thermometer (bottom).

enough (see figure 3.7). The only reliable temperature reading for a hypothermic victim is one obtained rectally. Conscious victims may be reluctant to allow their temperature to be taken in this manner, but they must be convinced that the reading provides important information.

Response

Hypothermia affects rescue techniques in several ways. Circulatory changes that affect blood volume and pressure create the need to remove the victim from the water horizontally to prevent circulatory collapse (Golden, Hervey, and Tipton 1991). Circulatory changes that affect the heart produce another absolute requirement—to handle the victim as gently as possible. Rough handling can cause the heart to fibrillate—a life-threatening condition in which the heart quivers, but does not contract. Even tugging wet clothing from a hypothermic victim can cause fibrillation. Use trauma shears to cut away wet clothing (see figure 3.8). Treat cold victims as though they were made of glass. Use the gentlest method possible to remove a hypothermic victim from the water. Do not allow cold, conscious victims to help extricate themselves from the water. Keep them horizontal and encourage them to minimize movement.

A rescuer may face a dilemma. A victim with a possible spinal cord injury should be immobilized before being removed from the water. If the victim is not breathing or is hypothermic and the water is cold, however, the rescue must be expedited. It would be a mistake to tow a victim with a possible spinal injury to shallow water if the water is cold. Moving the victim in the water accelerates heat loss. A paralyzed victim will be horizontal and have the head immersed, which nearly doubles heat loss. Do the best you can to minimize movement of

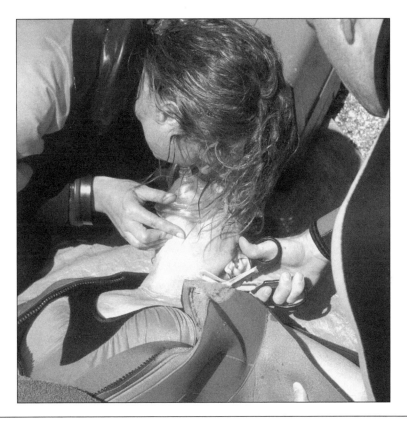

Figure 3.8 Place trauma shears at the top in your first aid equipment and use them to remove wet clothing as soon as possible.

the head, neck, and spine, but get such victims out of cold water quickly (see chapters 4 and 5).

First Aid

First aid procedures differ for mild and severe hypothermia (see table 3.2 and figure 3.9). The best way to differentiate initially is to observe whether the person is shivering. A person suffering from mild heat loss can shiver, but the victim of severe hypothermia is not capable of shivering.

If you have a hypothermic thermometer and the victim will cooperate, measure the person's core temperature rectally. Body temperature should increase about one degree Fahrenheit per hour. Prolonged shivering is to be expected and is a good sign. Just because the victim stops shivering and begins to feel better, however, does not mean that all is well. Keep checking the body core temperature until it reaches normal. If you are unable to measure core temperature accurately, the only reliable indicator of adequate warming is perspiration, which indicates excess body heat. The victim should avoid repeated exposure to cold for at least 24 hours.

Table 3.2   Key Points for Mild Hypothermia Treatment

Do	Don't
Stop further heat loss	Apply external heat
Handle the person gently	Massage the victim's extremities
Move the victim to a warm environment	Allow the victim to walk or exercise
Keep the victim horizontal	Elevate the victim's feet and legs
Cut away wet clothing and dry the victim	Attempt to rewarm the victim with body-to-body contact
Insulate with warm blankets and cover the head and neck	Allow stimulants (alcohol, caffeine, tobacco, drugs)
Allow tepid drinks (water or broth)	Allow hot drinks

Figure 3.9   The key to mild hypothermia first aid is insulating the victim and retaining body heat.

Use the procedures described later in this chapter for victims suffering from severe hypothermia. The victim will not be shivering and will be stiff and have bluish skin color. Breathing and pulse rates will be slow, the pupils of the eyes will respond slowly to light, and the person may be semiconscious or unconscious. Assess breathing and pulse for about 30 seconds. If breathing is absent, begin rescue breathing. If the pulse is absent, begin CPR unless the victim's chest is frozen or the person has been submerged for more than 60 minutes (National Safety Council 1997). Table 3.3 and figure 3.10 show the emergency medical care that should be provided to a severely hypothermic patient.

Problems with body-to-body warming attempts include insufficient heat, surface-area contact, and heat transfer. Also, skin warming slows core warming because elevated skin temperature signals the body to stop shivering, and

Table 3.3   Key Points for Severe Hypothermia Treatment

Do	Don't
Handle the victim as gently as possible	Attempt to rewarm the victim with warm water immersion
Keep the airway clear (suction or roll the victim to side)	Attempt fluids by mouth
Cut away clothing and dry and cover the victim (equal priority to resuscitation)	Attempt to rewarm the victim with body-to-body contact
Measure and document the core temperature (avoid if heat loss increased)	Apply external heat unless more than 30 minutes to the hospital
Evacuate by airlift	

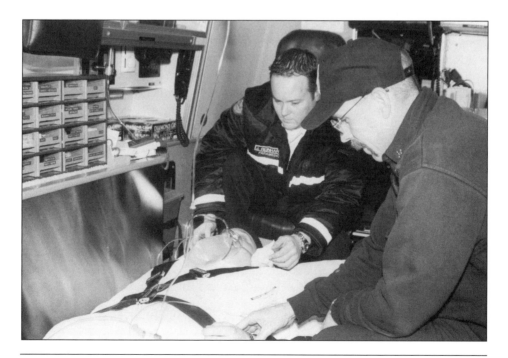

Figure 3.10   Victims of severe hypothermia are incapable of warming themselves and require medical care.

- Rapid transport to a medical facility
- Intubation of unresponsive victim
- Administration of heated and humidified oxygen
- Heated intravenous fluids
- Intravenous glucose
- Cardiac monitoring and possible defibrillation (defibrillation difficult)
- Core heating
- Blood acid control

Figure 3.11   Advanced medical care for the severely hypothermic individual.

shivering produces vital heat (National Safety Council 1997). If you are applying heat externally because of delayed treatment, be sure to apply hot packs or hot towels to large blood vessels that lie close to the skin on the neck, in the armpits, and at the creases of the legs in the groin. Figure 3.11 lists important items in the advanced medical care of the severely hypothermic victim; these may occur after initial emergency treatment.

Minimizing Hypothermia Risk

IN 1995 MY FIRE STATION RECEIVED A CALL to assist a 60-year-old male whose canoe had overturned about one-quarter mile from shore near Camano Island, Washington. Our rescue vessels were launched within eight minutes. Unfortunately, the man had attempted to swim to shore instead of clinging to his capsized canoe. He made it halfway. He was unconscious and unresponsive when retrieved from the water and did not survive the event. I believe that he would have been rescued and lived if he had just remained with the canoe until help arrived.

Individuals at high risk for hypothermia should avoid hazardous situations. High-risk people include the young, the elderly, the ill, and the intoxicated. The following actions have been proven to help reduce the loss of precious body heat in people who are suddenly immersed in cold water:

- Avoid drinking alcoholic beverages when in, on, or around water.
- Avoid tobacco use when in, on, or around water.
- Wear insulation.
- Keep clothing and footwear on if immersed.

- Keep the head out of water (wear a personal flotation device).
- Keep as still as possible. Use the heat-escape-lessening position (HELP) or huddle close together with others.
- Move with moving, cold water. Hanging onto a fixed object greatly increases heat loss.

Stimulants such as caffeine or nicotine affect circulation and increase heat loss. Clothing and footwear, including waders and boots, trap water next to the skin and, if movement does not exchange the water, decrease heat loss. Shielding high heat loss areas helps the body retain the heat it is producing. It is a myth that waders and clothing cause a person to sink. Apparel should be removed only if it hinders an exit from the water.

Attempting to swim to safety in cold water can be a fatal mistake if the distance is more than about 50 yards. Exercise in cold water increases body cooling by as much as 50 percent (Jacobs 1998). Activity flushes cold water through protective clothing and increases circulation to the extremities, which lose heat rapidly. Swimming and treading water accelerate heat loss and decrease survival time. Personal flotation will keep the head above water without swimming movements, and use of the heat-escape-lessening position (HELP) shown in figure 3.12 will help reduce heat loss. The goal is to protect the areas of the body where large blood vessels carry blood close to the surface—the neck, the wrists, and the groin where the legs bend.

Do not remove clothing when thrust unexpectedly into cold water. It is a myth that shoes or clothing will cause you to sink. If you retain your clothing and remain still, water inside your clothing and footwear will increase in temperature, and if stagnant, will reduce heat loss. Air trapped inside your clothing

Figure 3.12 The purpose of the heat-escape-lessening position (HELP) is to minimize heat loss from critical areas that include the abdomen, groin, and armpits.

can also provide buoyancy (see figure 3.13). The chart in table 3.4, with data gathered by the Recreational Boating Institute, provides a graphic comparison of immersion survival times.

Remember that water conducts heat about 25 times faster than air, so get out of the water no matter how cold the air temperature is. Do not abandon a capsized vessel until the vessel abandons you. Wind chill makes people feel cold, so they often go back into the water thinking that they will be warmer. They are reacting to skin temperature and do not realize that they are losing core body heat at a rapid rate. It is better to be miserable out of the water than to die in it.

Figure 3.13 Clothing can trap air and provide insulation, so it should not be removed until after exiting the water.

Table 3.4   Immersion Survival Times

Technique	Survival time in 50-degree-Fahrenheit water
HELP position	4 hours, 10 minutes
Huddling together	4 hours
Motionless with PFD	2 hours, 15 minutes
Treading water	*1 hour, 45 minutes
Swimming	*1 hour, 15 minutes
Drown-proofing	*1 hour

*Data for young, healthy male subjects. The average person lasts only half as long.

Half of the heat loss from the entire body occurs through the head in cold water. A major problem with swimming in cold water is that it requires energy to keep the head above water. Without flotation, exhaustion occurs quickly unless the head is immersed while swimming. And if the head is immersed, incapacitation from heat loss occurs quickly. Your best bet is to wear a personal flotation device, remain still, and keep your head above water. Drown-proofing—a survival technique intended to conserve energy in which the victim floats motionless with the face in the water and lifts the head to breathe occasionally—is a helpful survival technique for warm water, but detrimental in cold water.

Hyperthermia

Hyperthermia is the condition that results when a person's body core temperature rises above normal. The condition may be mild or severe. Hot water in contact with the body is the fastest way to elevate body temperature. A mild state of shock occurs when the body core temperature reaches 102 degrees Fahrenheit. When body temperature continues to escalate, heat stroke—severe hyperthermia—occurs (at a temperature of about 105 degrees Fahrenheit). Heat stroke is a life-threatening emergency with mortality rates of 20 to 70 percent (Mistovich et al. 2000). Figure 3.14 lists predisposing factors for body heat retention.

Physiology

A high body core temperature can cause several problems, especially when the temperature increases rapidly or when alcohol or drug use are a factor. Immersion in hot water increases body temperature quickly. High heat can cause drowsiness, loss of consciousness, and drowning. The U.S. Consumer Product Safety Commission (1994c) reports over 700 spa- and hot tub–related drowning deaths over the past 20 years. For victims affected by alcohol or drugs, the combination of a rapid increase in core temperature and a decrease in judgment may make them more likely to suffer the ultimate consequence of

- Hot environment (especially hot water)
- High humidity (greater than 75%)
- Age extremes (less than 6 years; more than 60 years)
- Medical conditions (e.g., diabetes)
- Physical structure (large or obese)

Figure 3.14 Hyperthermia risk factors.

The practical risk of hyperthermia begins in water warmer than 90 degrees Fahrenheit.

Figure 3.15 Consuming alcohol in a hot tub or spa increases the likelihood of an accident.

immersion hyperthermia. The combination of alcohol consumption, a hot tub, and prolonged immersion (more than 15 minutes) can be a recipe for disaster (see figure 3.15).

Heat Stroke

Mild hyperthermia results from excess fluid loss (sweating). The victim's skin is pale. The person feels weak, thirsty, and possibly dizzy. Muscle cramps may result from salts lost with sweat. Severe hyperthermia—heat stroke—results when a victim's body temperature–regulating mechanism fails and the body cannot dispose of excess heat. The victim's skin will be red and hot (check the forehead). Confusion, loss of consciousness, and dilated pupils are common signs. Seizures may occur. Heat stroke is an extreme medical emergency. Immediate first aid and prompt medical care are essential to minimize permanent damage to the brain.

Seizures

A sudden increase in body core temperature may cause seizures, which could be fatal if they occur while a person is immersed in water.

Birth Defects

Dr. James Ferguson of the University of Virginia Health Services Center warns that high heat during the first trimester of a pregnancy may cause birth defects. The U.S. Consumer Product Safety Commission (1994c) recommends that pregnant women and young children not use a spa or hot tub before consulting with a physician.

Recognition

Signs and symptoms of heat illnesses include pale skin, dizziness, nausea, vomiting, thirst, confusion, and loss of consciousness. Victims may experience seizures. Anyone who looks or feels bad should be assisted from or removed from hot water.

Response

Owners of hot tubs or whirlpools should know where the cutoff switch is for the pump and teach family members how to turn off the power to the pump. Be alert for signs of altered mental status—ranging from confusion to loss of consciousness—and remove victims from the spa, hot tub, or whirlpool. Keep a pair of scissors nearby to cut entangled hair in an emergency.

First Aid

A conscious victim will feel weak, lightheaded, and nauseous. Table 3.5 and figure 3.16 describe the various first aid responses for victims of hyperthermia.

Table 3.5   Key Points for Hyperthermia Treatment

For mild hyperthermia	For severe hyperthermia*	
Do	Do	Don't
Move the victim to a cool environment	Move the victim to a cool environment	Elevate the victim's feet and legs
Place the victim in a horizontal position	Place the victim in a horizontal position	Attempt oral fluid intake
Elevate the victim's feet and legs	Assess breathing and circulation and initiate resuscitation as needed	
Measure body temperature (standard thermometer orally)	Cover the victim with a wet sheet and fan	
Apply wet compresses to the head, neck, armpits, and groin	Apply wrapped cold packs to the head, neck, armpits, and groin	
Allow the victim to drink cool noncaffeinated liquids	If you suspect a submersion injury, send a water sample to the medical facility with the victim (a laboratory analysis of the fluid will aid in the treatment of the patient).	

*When the victim has an altered mental status or is unconscious.

Figure 3.16 Victims of mild hyperthermia respond quickly to cooling, but must avoid repeating the activity that caused the problem initially.

Advanced medical care of the hyperthermic victim may include the use of high-flow supplemental oxygen, intravenous fluids if the patient is unable to take liquids orally, intravenous glucose, and cardiac monitoring.

Minimizing Hyperthermia Risk

Water temperature in hot tubs and spas should not be raised above 104 degrees Fahrenheit. Alcohol consumption should be avoided before and while using a spa or hot tub. Immersion duration times should not be prolonged. Users should exit the water at the first indication of overheating (e.g., weakness, nausea, and so on). Young children using spas and hot tubs should have advance approval and guidelines for use from a physician and must be supervised constantly. Keep in mind that temperature-related problems occur faster in children than in adults. How you feel is not a reliable guide for how your children feel. One-third of the victims of hot tubs and spas are children under the age of five. A locked safety cover on a hot tub or spa when it is not being used is essential. Constant adult supervision also is essential when a hot tub or spa is in use. Hair entanglement in the suction fitting of a spa, hot tub, or whirlpool can hold a victim underwater. Drain covers should be used to reduce the risk of hair entanglement. Dome-shaped drain outlets help prevent body part entrapment caused by suction.

Key Points

Water has great ability to add or remove heat rapidly from the human body. Hypothermia and hyperthermia are the lowering and raising of body core temperature, respectively. Either condition may range from mild to severe. Anything that affects circulation and body metabolism increases a person's risk for these conditions. Some people—especially children and the elderly—can survive prolonged submersion in cold water. Sudden immersion in cold water may cause several life-threatening physiological reactions. Swimming or treading in cold water is ill advised because the activity accelerates body heat loss. Wearing a personal flotation device to keep the head above water while remaining still and bunching up the body to shield high-loss areas are desirable actions. Hypothermia requires specific rescue techniques to help prevent circulatory collapse and heart rhythm irregularities. Both hypo- and hyperthermia must be identified. Victims must be handled and positioned correctly. Advanced medical care and rapid transport to a medical facility are essential for severe cases. Knowledge and its correct application are paramount for the prevention of excess heat loss or heat retention.

Chapter 4

Heart, Lung, and Head Injuries

This chapter will address immersion and submersion injuries that involve the heart, lungs, and brain. Identifying potential health problems through regular physical examinations and avoiding strenuous aquatic activities when known problems exist can prevent most of these injuries.

A MIDDLE-AGED MAN, WHOM WE WILL CALL EARL, was completing scuba diving training in England. The water was cold, and Earl was not in the best physical condition. During a training dive, a scuba instructor checked Earl's air pressure and found that his tank was about half full. The instructor then signaled for the class to turn around and proceed back toward the exit point. A couple of minutes later Earl swam in front of the instructor and signaled frantically that he was out of air. The instructor attempted to provide air via a secondary scuba regulator, but Earl rejected the device. The instructor had Earl in his grasp and was attempting to swim him to the surface when Earl lost consciousness and caused both himself and the instructor to sink. The instructor swam harder and inflated his dry suit to increase buoyancy. The combination of the swimming efforts, the buoyancy, and Earl's weight caused the scuba instructor to lose his grasp and shoot quickly to the surface while Earl sank to the bottom. When Earl was recovered, he could not be resuscitated. The medical examiner ruled the cause of death as drowning. The conclusion is correct, but the medical examiner did not identify the true cause of the accident—pulmonary distress caused by cardiac inadequacies, which I will explain later in this chapter.

MY WIFE AND I HAD ENJOYED OUR SCUBA DIVING VACATIONS with Gary, a scuba instructor and tour organizer from St. Louis, Missouri. One day I received a long-distance phone call. The caller said, "You were a friend of Gary's, weren't you?" Shocked, I said, "Yes, why?" The caller informed me that Gary had been diving at a depth of 80 feet in Belize when suddenly he had stopped swimming and gone limp in the water. He was rescued immediately and resuscitation was attempted, but to no avail. An autopsy revealed the cause of death as a ruptured blood vessel in his brain. Gary's accident was not preventable because he did not have a history of circulatory problems, but many such accidents can be prevented. Loss of circulation to the brain (stroke or brain attack) and loss of circulation to the heart (heart attack) obviously are more life threatening when they occur during immersion (head above water) or submersion (completely submerged). Heart rhythm irregularities under such conditions also cause fatalities.

Learning Goals   *By the end of this chapter, you should be able to:*

- State two ways to minimize submersion injuries that involve prior heart, lung, and brain medical problems.
- Define and explain the sudden death syndrome.
- List 8 of 11 cardiovascular stresses that contribute to sudden death syndrome.
- List 5 of 7 controllable factors that contribute to arterial disease.
- Contrast a massive heart attack and a classic heart attack.
- List the three major contributing factors that lead to pulmonary edema.
- Explain the cause of scuba diving lung overexpansion injuries.
- State the most important action to take for a victim of water aspiration.

- ▶ List three actions that should be taken to prevent aspiration of regurgitated stomach contents when a victim is unconscious.
- ▶ Contrast two types of stroke and list 7 of 10 signs and symptoms of stroke.
- ▶ State the best way to avoid neurological injuries from toxic marine creatures.
- ▶ State the principal problem resulting from aquatic ear injuries.
- ▶ Explain why the use of decongestants should be avoided before scuba diving.
- ▶ Describe how to position a victim who experiences a classic heart attack, a stroke, a seizure, or breathing difficulty.

Heart Injuries and Illnesses

The heart is a miraculous four-chamber pump that takes oxygen-depleted blood from the body, sends it through the lungs to eliminate carbon dioxide and acquire oxygen, and sends the oxygenated blood to tissues throughout the body (see figure 4.1). Electrical activity controls the rhythmic contractions of the heart (see

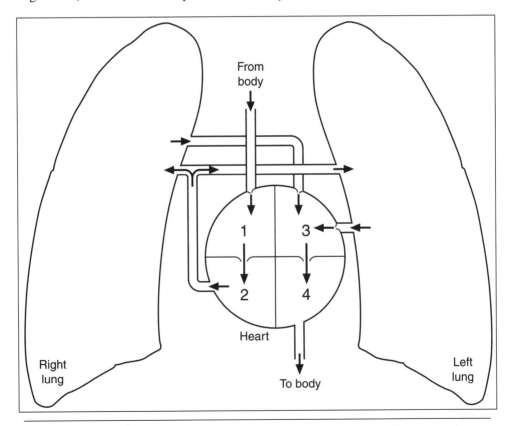

Figure 4.1 Deoxygenated blood from the body enters the right atrium (1) of the heart and passes through a valve into the right ventricle (2), where it is pumped into the lungs. Oxygenated blood returns from the lungs to the left atrium (3) and passes through a valve into the left ventricle (4), where it is pumped out to the body.

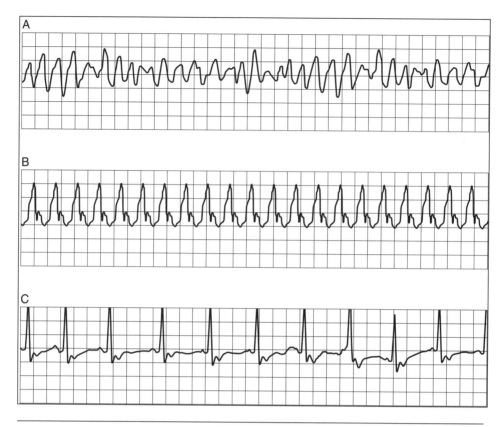

Figure 4.2 Potentially fatal cardiac rhythms *(A and B)* compared to a normal cardiac rhythm *(C)*. Potentially fatal rhythms may be induced by the stresses of an aquatic environment.

figure 4.2). It is an incredibly marvelous machine, but it can develop problems, especially when not cared for. Unhealthy habits cause arterial disease and can increase the workload of the heart or lead to the formation of a blood clot in a narrowed artery—a heart attack. Even seemingly healthy hearts can lose the synchronization of contractions and fibrillate (quiver out of rhythm without pumping blood) when certain factors in the aquatic environment combine to trigger an event that can be fatal. Loss of consciousness while immersed or submerged is deadly. A healthy heart that is cold does not pump as effectively as one at normal body temperature. Aquatic activities pose many cardiac concerns, but knowledge and good use of that knowledge can help prevent disasters.

It is not uncommon to find on scuba diving accident reports that the victim had a "minor" heart condition and that the deceased's physician had indicated that the problem should not prevent the person from participating in scuba diving activities. The average physician is not trained in diving medicine and does not understand the complexities of submersion physiology. Anyone who has a physical condition that is less than normal should consult with a diving doctor before taking a risk that could be fatal. Scuba diving is not for everyone.

It is a wonderful pursuit for people with good health, but it can kill individuals who think that they will be all right in spite of a medical condition. Even if the physician you have trusted for many years gives you medical authorization for scuba diving instruction, obtain approval from a physician trained in dive medicine before pursuing this endeavor if you have any health problems—especially those that are heart related. My personal opinion is that people with a history of heart problems should not scuba dive, period. Many other adventurous pursuits offer a much greater chance of survival to a person who loses consciousness. According to the Divers Alert Network annual report of dive injuries and fatalities, more than 10 percent of dive fatalities result from coronary problems that simply happen to occur while diving (Divers Alert Network 2001).

Sudden Death Syndrome

I HAD COLLECTED ACCIDENT REPORTS FOR SUDDEN DEATHS for years before meeting Bob Temple, a scuba instructor from Redmond, Washington, who was a monitor technician for heart scan devices. In a letter to the Undersea Hyperbaric and Medical Society proposing a study to monitor heart rhythms in scuba divers, Bob had written, "There are at present three to five occurrences each year of sudden, unexplained deaths while scuba diving; some occurring on the surface prior to the dive, others on the surface immediately following the dive. I thought initially that this phenomenon was gender and age specific, but I have discovered cases of males as young as 30 and a couple of cases involving females. I was able to review some autopsy reports and was appalled at the inconsistencies they contained. Applying what I had learned over the years pertaining to heart rhythms, it became apparent that not only were some autopsy reports inconclusive as to a cause of death based on witness testimony, others were just dead wrong."

Sudden death syndrome is a rapid onset of loss of circulation caused by the heart losing its rhythm (fibrillation) or stopping (arrest). A significant problem of the sudden death syndrome is the lack of symptoms to alert anyone. Heart rhythm irregularities cannot be detected by autopsy, and a heart attack cannot be detected unless it is massive or the victim lives at least six hours following the attack. The only good news from a review of literature on the subject of sudden deaths is from a Swiss study by Joki and Melzer, who concluded, "no death can be blamed on strenuous physical exertion on a healthy heart" (Joki and Melzer 1971).

Cardiac risk is greatest when a sedentary person suddenly engages in strenuous physical activity. Other cardiovascular stressors include excessive cold, fatigue, excessive workload, dehydration, poor physical fitness, physical and emotional stress, advanced age, lack of environmental protection suits, medicine or drug use, and tobacco use. Many of these factors may be present in an aquatic set-

Figure 4.3   Scuba diving in cold water places great stress on the cardiovascular system.

ting (see figure 4.3). Bachrach and Egstrom (1990) conclude in their combined paper that "the sensitivity of heart rate and rhythm to various stressors is acute, but it is likely that in no other activity does the combination of cardiovascular stresses exist that we encounter in diving."

Surawicz (1985) identified metabolic acidosis as a factor in cardiac rhythm irregularities. Acid reduces the threshold for fibrillation of the heart—the condition in which the heart goes out of rhythm and stops pumping. Strenuous exercise in cells that do not receive enough oxygen acidifies blood. The worst situation is anaerobic strenuous exercise (exercising in the absence of oxygen). These conditions exist in the cells of a person immersed for an extended period in cold water who begins struggling to reach the surface or in a diver who surfaces and must swim against a current.

Arterial Disease

Many factors can contribute to atherosclerosis (the accumulation of deposits inside the arteries) and arteriosclerosis (hardening of the arteries) (see figure 4.4). Factors that cannot be controlled are heredity, gender, age, and diseases. Controllable factors include high blood pressure, high cholesterol levels, obesity, smoking, stress, and physical inactivity. Both conditions are called "silent killers" because they progress so slowly that many victims are unaware that they exist until a tragedy occurs.

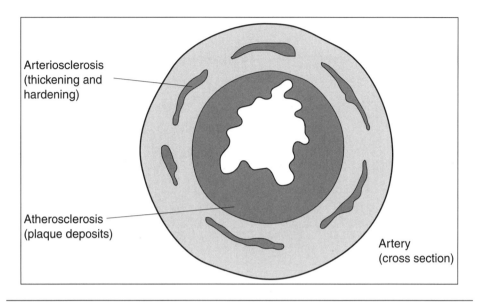

Arteriosclerosis
(thickening and
hardening)

Atherosclerosis
(plaque deposits)

Artery
(cross section)

Figure 4.4 Arterial disease can restrict the flow of blood and cause clotting that produces a heart attack or a stroke. The disease can also harden the arteries and cause high blood pressure.

Coronary artery disease causes heart attacks and heart rhythm disasters. Many people who think that they are perfectly healthy have occluded arteries in their hearts. The chart in figure 4.5 shows occlusion percentages for three individuals who died suddenly while scuba diving. These individuals were not aware of any existing heart problems.

- 65-year-old female from Texas with 40% occlusion of a coronary artery
- 48-year-old male from California with 60% occlusion of a coronary artery
- 31-year-old male from Florida with 90% occlusion of a coronary artery

Figure 4.5 Coronary occlusion percentages of sudden death victims.

Heart Attacks

Coronary artery disease leads to a heart attack when a blood clot forms in an occluded artery in the heart. If the interruption of circulation occurs in a large artery near the top of the heart, a massive heart attack occurs, the victim loses consciousness almost instantly, and resuscitation is extremely difficult. If the

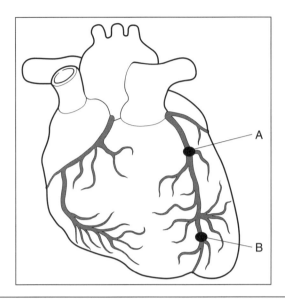

Figure 4.6   (**A**) A heart attack occurring in a large artery is classified as massive and causes immediate loss of consciousness; (**B**) a blockage in a smaller artery is a classic heart attack that causes chest pain.

clot forms in a smaller artery near the bottom of the heart, the result is a classic heart attack. Figure 4.6 illustrates these two examples of heart attacks. The victim of a classic heart attack experiences chest pain and remains conscious for a period of time. Eventually, irritation of the nerves and cells that cause the heart muscle to contract leads to ventricular fibrillation, loss of pulse, and loss of consciousness. The chances of survival are much better for a person experiencing a classical heart attack than are those for a person experiencing a massive heart attack, especially when defibrillation can be accomplished with an automatic external defibrillator (AED). Unfortunately, the availability of an AED at an aquatic setting is unlikely, and defibrillation is less effective when the victim is hypothermic.

A heart attack can incapacitate suddenly, and sudden incapacitation in water can lead to drowning. In spite of what the average physician may say about participation in active sports, an individual with a heart condition—even a minor one—should think seriously about the increased risk of heart problems posed by the aquatic environment before considering participation in a water sport, especially scuba diving. Heart attack problems for scuba divers are increased because divers breathe dehumidified air, which causes dehydration and blood thickening. Thicker blood is more likely to clot. Hypothermia also contributes to dehydration.

Heart Workload

Dr. C.E.G. Lundgren wrote in a paper presented at the International Symposium on Man in the Sea that "intrathoracic blood pooling (caused by submersion) increases venous filling of the heart, thereby inducing a 30 percent increase in cardiac output due to an increase in stroke volume" (Arborelius et al. 1972). The heart of a submerged person must work harder than normal. Following an initial rate increase, the heart rate of a person immersed in water tends to slow, especially if the person's face is immersed (Shepherd and Vanhoutte 1979). As the individual becomes colder, blood shunted from the extremities adds to the intrathoracic blood pooling caused by water pressure. The kidneys begin processing the increased volume and remove excess fluid (Golden, Tipton, and Scott 1997). The blood becomes thicker as the heart becomes cooler. In addition to the tendency toward dangerous rhythm abnormalities, the combined physiological changes just described can lead to pulmonary edema.

Lung Injuries and Illnesses

An individual immersed or submerged in water has more difficulty breathing (see figure 4.7). With each foot of depth in water, pressure increases slightly over 0.4 pounds per square foot. A person erect in water cannot take a full breath because the muscles of the diaphragm cannot overcome the water pressure

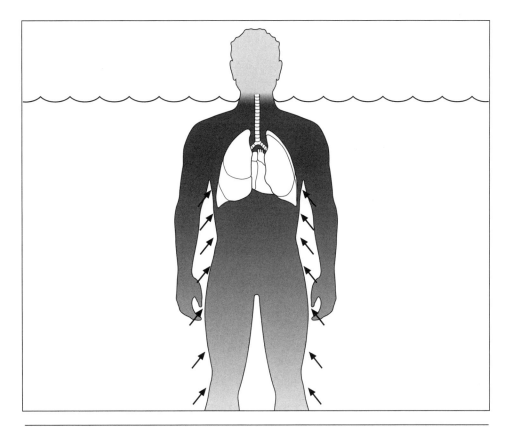

Figure 4.7 Water pressure on the body shifts blood upward, reduces lung volume, and increases the workload of the heart.

pushing up on the diaphragm. Moreover, as a result of the higher-than-normal blood volume output of the heart, the lungs contain more blood than normal, which also decreases lung volume slightly.

Pulmonary Edema

The combined effects of cold water and hydrostatic pressure can cause fluid to accumulate in the lungs. This occurs when the pressure within the blood vessels of the lungs causes an osmotic effect on the plasma in the blood; the watery fluid shifts from the blood vessels into the lungs. This condition, called pulmonary edema, may cause deaths that are classified as drowning. A paper from the London St. Thomas' Hospital Department of Cardiology states, "Water inhalation is not the only immersion injury that produces wet lungs. The effects of pulmonary edema and drowning appear identical, so pulmonary edema can be mistaken for near-drowning" (Wilmshurst et al. 1989). Cardiologists who studied scuba divers who had experienced pulmonary edema did not find cardiac problems in the test subjects. Instead, they found an abnormal response to cold and immersion and concluded that the problem stemmed from "abnormal vascular reactivity to physiological stimulation." Some people just react more strongly to cold and increased oxygen levels, which are both factors common to scuba diving (Wilmshurst et al. 1989).

During immersion and submersion episodes, symptoms and signs of pulmonary edema include breathing difficulty, heart palpitations, expectoration of bloody sputum, and syncope (fainting) (see table 4.1). The signs and symptoms often are mistaken for other extremely serious scuba diving injuries (see chapter 7). Many cases of mild to moderate pulmonary edema probably are not reported because most victims experience an improvement in breathing ability immediately upon leaving the water. Scuba divers also may fail to report the

Table 4.1   Unexplained Pulmonary Edema

Location	Description of problem	Signs
Surface	Shortness of breath	Pale, coughing up bloody froth
Surface	Hyperventilating	Loss of consciousness
Surface	Difficulty breathing	Pale, coughing
10 feet under water	Difficulty breathing	Loss of consciousness after surfacing
Surface	Feels exhausted	Incapacitated
Surface	Hyperventilating	Loss of consciousness
Surface	Difficulty breathing	Noisy breath sounds
Surface	Difficulty breathing	Loss of consciousness
Surface after dive	Difficulty breathing	Coughing up bloody froth

problem because dive sites are remote from medical facilities and because they fear being banned from future diving activities.

Fortunately, acute (sudden-onset) pulmonary edema does not affect people with normal physiological responses, does not affect swimmers, and only occurs in water colder than 54 degrees Fahrenheit. New or novice scuba divers would do well to consider the recipe for disaster spelled out in figure 4.8, and to remember that pulmonary edema can lead to loss of consciousness and drowning.

If a person's heart is not completely normal and strong, pulmonary edema is even more likely to occur. Earl, the Englishman in the opening story in this chapter, experienced difficulty and lost consciousness from pulmonary edema. Ultimately, he drowned, but the reason that he drowned is that he was unable to obtain enough oxygen to remain conscious because he was exerting and had fluid in his lungs. It is my opinion that in many cases in which a scuba diver reported that his buddy signaled "out of air," the victim was merely unable to breathe because of pulmonary edema.

Moving in the dense medium of water requires significantly more energy than moving in air. Doubling swimming speed in water requires an eightfold energy (and oxygen) increase. Strenuous exertion in water places heavy demands on the heart and lungs. Individuals who panic and struggle in water become exhausted quickly. The average person struggles for less than one minute before succumbing. Excessive exertion in water must be avoided.

> - 1 large body of cold water (below 54 degrees Fahrenheit)
> - 1 cooled heart
> - 1 predisposition to increased vascular resistance when cold and immersed
> - Place individual into body of water briefly.
> - Remove when breathing becomes difficult.

Figure 4.8 Recipe for acute pulmonary edema.
Using an out-of-shape individual may accelerate the process.

Other Scuba Diving Lung Problems

As pressure increases with depth, air spaces become compressed, including those in the lungs. To keep the lungs at normal volume, a scuba regulator delivers air at a pressure equal to the depth of the water. All is well unless a diver panics, instinctively holds his breath, and bolts to the surface. As the surrounding pressure decreases during ascent, air in the lungs of the scuba diver tries to expand. When the lungs cannot expand any more, they rupture. Air from the lungs escapes into the chest and possibly into the circulatory system. The ruptured lung may collapse. Air may be trapped in the middle of the chest or migrate along the breastbone to the base of the neck. A ruptured lung is obviously a serious medical condition. If the victim does not lose consciousness from air bubbles obstructing circulation to the brain (see the section on brain attack and air embolism later in this chapter), some of the following signs and symptoms may be present:

- Breathing difficulty
- Chest pain
- Coughing
- Pallor
- Air under the skin
- Voice change
- Swallowing difficulty
- Leaning to one side
- Unequal chest expansion
- Tracheal deviation

Lung barotrauma (pressure-related injury) during ascent also may be caused by air trapped in the lungs from asthma, mucus plugs, or a spasm of the larynx from aspirated water. Figure 4.9 depicts other forms of lung trauma associated with scuba diving.

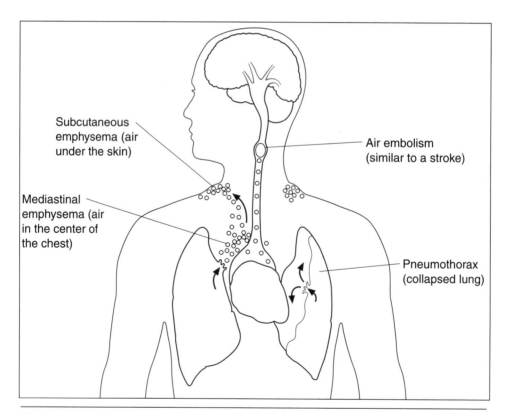

Figure 4.9 Holding the breath during ascent after breathing compressed air can rupture the lungs and force air into other parts of the body.

Nitrogen, an inert gas that comprises more than three-quarters of the air we breathe, is absorbed into the body's blood and tissues while scuba diving. A diver who limits time at depth and ascends slowly does not experience any problems from the dissolved nitrogen. Divers who remain at depth too long and ascend too quickly, however, are likely to develop decompression illness in which the excess dissolved gas comes out of solution in the form of bubbles. The effect is similar to carbon dioxide dissolved under pressure in soda. When the pressure is reduced quickly by opening the container, bubbles form. Bubbles are good in soda, but bad in divers. The bubbles can affect many tissues in the body including the brain, the spinal cord, and the lungs. Bubbles trapped within the tiny blood vessels of the lungs can cause a condition known as the "chokes." The victim will cough, have difficulty breathing, and may lose consciousness.

Distinguishing among various lung problems can be difficult because they produce similar signs and symptoms. Fortunately, the first aid procedures are the same for all conditions that cause respiratory distress or arrest.

Asthma

Asthma is a pulmonary problem that can be triggered by many factors common to the aquatic environment: cold, stress, exertion, and breathing dry air from a scuba tank. Spasm of the bronchioles (subdivisions of the bronchial tubes in the lungs) can develop rapidly, trapping air within the lungs. Breathing difficulty while in the water may cause victims of asthma attacks to panic.

THE THIN YOUNG WOMAN CLUNG DESPERATELY to the straps on my scuba tank while I backed out of the ocean at Santa Barbara, California. She was a student in my scuba class and was participating in her first training dive. She had appeared distressed following our surface swim out to the dive site, so I approached her and asked her what was wrong. She did not reply. Strange breath sounds indicated a problem. I increased her buoyancy, reassured her, instructed the class to follow me, and pushed the woman to shallow water. It was a struggle to get her through the surf zone because she was unable to help, but we succeeded. When I finally got her ashore, she rested, recovered somewhat, and told me that she had asthma. She had to complete a medical history questionnaire at the beginning of the course, and the form asked about asthma, but she had not checked the adjacent box. I asked her why she had not disclosed her condition. She said, "I knew that if I told you that I was asthmatic that you would not allow me to take the class." She was right!

A couple of years later a man taking a scuba instructor course that I was directing experienced similar problems during a rescue exercise. After assisting him to shore, I didn't wait for an explanation. "Why didn't you tell me that you had asthma?" I asked. His reply was exactly what I expected: "You wouldn't have allowed me to take the instructor course if I had told you about my asthma." He was right also.

People with medical conditions that can be aggravated by aquatic conditions must use common sense and avoid placing themselves in jeopardy needlessly. There are many other exciting endeavors in which the participant is not subjected to the stresses of cold and pressure.

Water Aspiration

Aspiration of water without submersion can cause injury even though the victim may not lose consciousness. Scuba divers and snorkelers may breathe small amounts of water because of faulty equipment. Surfers also experience the problem with the spray from large waves, and people rescued by helicopter may suffer the malady because of the spray created by the powerful downdraft of the aircraft's rotor. Water in the lungs can dilute surfactant, a protein substance that reduces surface tension and helps prevent the tiny air sacs in the lungs from collapsing during exhalation. When the air sacs collapse, breathing difficulty increases. Severe complications, including death, may follow. People emerging from the water who display the signs and symptoms listed in figure 4.10 should be kept still and warm and taken to a medical facility. Symptoms may persist from one hour to many days. Medical care is essential (see figure 4.11).

Regurgitation Aspiration

The airway is the path from the nose and mouth that air travels through to reach the lung. Air passes through the throat, larynx, windpipe, and bronchial tubes. Figure 4.12 illustrates an airway with aspiration problems. Conscious people have muscle tone and reflexes and are able to maintain an open airway and protect against the aspiration of fluids by means of a cough reflex and spasm

Coughing followed later by the following:

- Tremors or shivering
- Hot or cold sensations
- Nausea, vomiting, or both

Generalized aching followed one to two hours later by the following:

- Breathing difficulty
- More coughing
- Sputum
- Chest pain
- Loss of appetite

Figure 4.10 Signs and symptoms of water aspiration.

Figure 4.11 Any person who has lost consciousness while in water must receive medical attention, but it is common for victims to reject the recommendation because of embarrassment. Be persuasive.

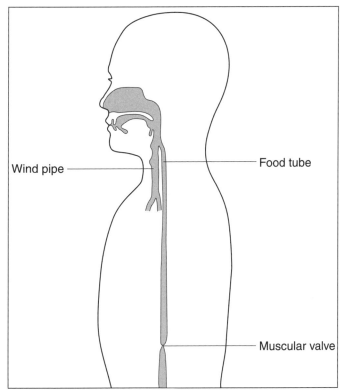

Wind pipe

Food tube

Muscular valve

Figure 4.12 Unconscious victims lack muscle tone and reflexes and can aspirate fluid, which can be fatal. Fluids from the stomach can get into the lungs via the windpipe. Maintaining a clear airway is of paramount importance.

of the larynx. Unconscious people lack muscle tone and reflexes and face life-threatening airway problems. The problem is even more complex for the victim of a submersion injury. Basic CPR training teaches that the first action in caring for a victim (after checking for responsiveness and summoning help) is to establish an airway. Many people who have completed CPR training still do not fully understand airway problems. They check for breathing in an unconscious victim without opening the airway, and they often check for circulation before opening the airway and checking for breathing. CPR priorities are (1) airway, (2) breathing, and (3) circulation—in that order (think of it as ABC).

After taking steps to open the airway (keeping in mind that a spinal cord injury must be considered until it can definitely be ruled out), ensure that the airway is clear. Victims of submersion injuries swallow large amounts of water. With muscles in the esophagus relaxed from lack of oxygen, stomach contents can regurgitate into the throat. If the airway is not clear and the victim breathes or receives rescue breaths, the fluid can be aspirated or blown into the lungs. The fatality rate for aspiration of stomach regurgitation is high! Keep the airway clear. Examine the mouth and throat before initiating rescue breathing, and listen to air movement sounds during rescue breathing. A gurgling sound indicates fluid in the airway. It is essential to keep the airway clear during resuscitation (see chapter 9) to protect the lungs.

Allergic Reactions

When a person's immune system is sensitized, exposure to a substance to which the person is allergic can cause a life-threatening reaction known as anaphylaxis. The blood vessels in the body relax while the airways in the lungs constrict. Respiratory distress and severe shock develop rapidly and death can occur unless intervention is immediate. In the aquatic environment, allergic reaction is most likely to result from animal venom, such as the sting of a jellyfish or cone shell in tropical waters. Signs and symptoms include breathing difficulty; wheezing; swollen lips, tongue, throat, and vocal cords; skin welts; seizures; and abnormal heart rhythms. The victim's condition can deteriorate rapidly. Emergency medical assistance is vital.

A person also may develop an allergic reaction from something ingested just prior to entering the water. Medications, shellfish consumption, or the ingestion of anything to which the person is sensitized can produce the condition. The victim of an allergic reaction in the water must be rescued quickly. Incapacitation will occur rapidly.

Head Injuries and Illnesses

Types of head injuries include brain attack (stroke), air embolism, and ear damage. Aquatic activities may cause these events to culminate when a problem has existed for years. Head injuries tend to be sudden and debilitating and can lead to loss of consciousness and drowning. A seizure is not an injury, but may result from an injury or a variety of causes. Seizures also incapacitate people and are a principal cause of drowning for individuals who are prone to them.

Brain Attack and Air Embolism

A new term for a stroke is *brain attack*, which occurs from an occluded or ruptured cerebral artery. The medical term for the condition is *cerebrovascular accident*, or *CVA*. Occlusion brain attacks are the most common and usually are caused by the same factors that lead to heart attacks, although a scuba diver who is completely healthy can suffer an instantaneous brain attack when an air bubble obstructs an artery in the brain (see figure 4.13). When air escapes from a ruptured lung (see the section on lung injuries and illnesses in this chapter) and enters the circulatory system, the gas is likely to go through the heart and move up the arteries to the brain. As the diameter of an artery becomes smaller than the diameter of the bubble, the bubble will lodge in the artery and obstruct circulation. This condition is known as an air embolism. Exertion may cause an aneurysm—an abnormal dilatation of a weakened cerebral artery—to burst and produce a CVA. Brain attacks may be temporary, mild, or severe. These events can be disorienting, disabling, and deadly to anyone engaged in an aquatic activity. Air embolisms and cerebrovascular accidents are both extremely serious medical conditions.

Signals of a brain attack and air embolism include confusion, loss of balance, visual disturbances, and abnormalities on one side of the body. The pupils of the eyes may be unequal sizes. Other serious signs include speech problems, loss of the ability to swallow, loss of consciousness, seizures, and respiratory or cardiac arrest. The indications may disappear within seconds or may persist indefinitely. Medical attention is crucial following any signs of brain attack, no matter how brief in duration, because the body is indicating that a more significant event may be imminent. Any person who loses consciousness while in water must also be evaluated at a medical facility.

Controllable factors that predispose a person to brain attacks include high blood pressure, dehydration, obesity, cigarette smoking, alcohol consumption,

- Cigarette smoking
- High blood pressure
- High blood cholesterol
- Lack of exercise
- Obesity
- Heart disease
- Transient ischemic attacks (mini-strokes)

Figure 4.13 Causes of brain attack.

and stimulant drugs. Although we can control blood pressure and hydration on land, remember that immersion increases blood pressure and causes dehydration. And always keep in mind the terrible effects of the excessive loss of body heat. The risk of a brain attack is increased in the aquatic environment, so individuals who are at risk should be particularly cautious. Uncontrollable factors that predispose people to brain attacks include diseases, advanced age, and family history (American Heart Association 1999, 42).

Seizures

Seizures are another severe brain problem. They range from mild (petit mal) to severe (grand mal), may last from seconds to several minutes, and may be singular or multiple. The condition is not just a result of epilepsy. A grand mal seizure occurring while immersed or submerged is likely to be fatal. In addition to a brain attack and epilepsy, seizures may be caused by the following (Limmer et al. 2001):

- Low blood sugar
- Drug overdose
- Poisoning
- Infection
- Head injury (from previous accident common)
- Low oxygen levels
- Anaphylaxis
- Hysteria
- Pregnancy
- Shock
- Breathing above-normal oxygen concentrations while submerged (oxygen toxicity)
- Undetermined reasons (idiopathic)

People with seizure disorders, especially those who have had recent changes in their prescribed anticonvulsant medications, are at four to five times increased risk of submersion injuries (Weinstein and Krieger 1996). Individuals with a history of seizures should engage in aquatic activities—including bathing—only under the close, continuous supervision of individuals who are trained rescuers and CPR providers. People with seizure disorders account for more than half of all drownings in bathtubs (Patetta et al. 1986).

Healthy scuba divers can experience seizures without warning. Breathing pure oxygen at depths greater than 25 feet, breathing enriched air nitrox (EAN) at depths beyond 100 feet, or breathing mixed gases at greater depths can cause oxygen toxicity, which produces grand mal seizures with sudden onset.

Neurological Injuries

Stings from venomous marine life can cause life-threatening injuries because they affect the body's neurological system. Injuries from animals such as jellyfish, lionfish, moray eel, scorpion fish, stingray, and stonefish can be deadly (see figure 4.14, *a-f*). Stings from several ocean creatures require an antivenin. Some marine life wounds that would be minor injuries for the average person can produce life-threatening allergic reactions in some victims. A person suffering a severe allergic reaction requires immediate treatment with epinephrine (adrenaline).

Figure 4.14 Many marine animals can inflict venomous stings and wounds that can cause life-threatening emergencies. Be prepared for injuries that can occur in specific geographic areas, especially remote locations.

Neurotoxins can cause paralysis, breathing difficulty, and respiratory arrest. Rescue breathing and CPR may be required. Immediate transport to a medical facility equipped to manage marine life injuries is essential. Additional first aid procedures for venomous stings are contained in chapter 9.

Venomous marine animals are colorful or unusual. Injuries usually occur when people handle or provoke the creatures. Unintentional contact when wading or swimming also causes injuries, especially from stingrays and jellyfish. The key to prevention is to avoid contact. Wear an exposure suit for protection from sunburn, heat loss, and stings. Shuffle your feet along the bottom when wading in shallow seawater. Avoid handling or provoking animals.

Ear Injuries

Several types of ear injuries can result from submersion. Hearing ability may be affected, but the immediate concern is the injured person's equilibrium. The inner ear contains semicircular canals (see figure 4.15) that help establish orientation. Trauma to the inner ear can affect balance and orientation and cause vertigo and disorientation.

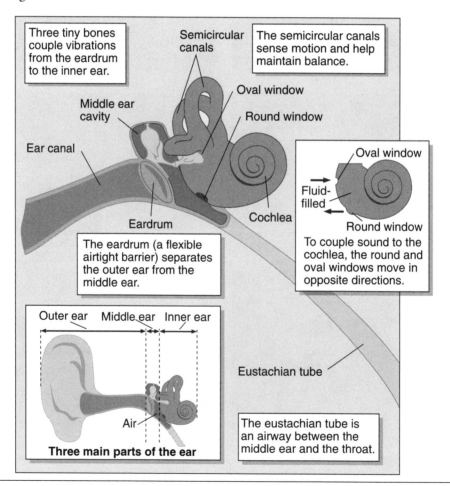

Figure 4.15 Ear anatomy.

Adapted, by permission, from D.K. Graver, 2003, *Scuba Diving*, 3rd edition (Champaign, IL: Human Kinetics), 99.

Surface ear injuries occur when a person strikes water at high velocity, such as a water skier who falls. When the ear strikes the water forcibly, a shock wave into the ear canal can cause substantial damage to the middle ear and inner ear.

Underwater ear injuries occur when swimmers and skin and scuba divers fail to maintain equal pressure between the middle ear and the outer ear. Divers learn various techniques to open the eustachian tubes that connect the throat and middle ear. Opening the tubes allows air pressure in the throat, which is equal to the surrounding pressure, to equalize with the pressure in the middle ear. Failure to equalize the pressure can result in a painful condition called a squeeze. Failure to correct a squeeze may lead to a perforation of the eardrum. When cold water rushes through the breach in the eardrum and contacts the inner ear, vertigo results from unequal temperatures in the organs of balance. The vertigo can be incapacitating. A diver experiencing the problem must remain still and calm until the water in the ear warms and orientation returns. Divers may panic when they experience pain and vertigo. Prevention of the injury is easy and paramount and is a key concept during scuba instruction.

Unequal pressures or temperatures in the inner ear can cause disorientation. Cold water entering only one ear canal may cause vertigo. Individuals with ear-wax accumulation in one ear may experience this difficulty. Scuba divers who wear insulating hoods to reduce heat loss are also candidates for the problem if water seeps into one ear and not the other.

Scuba divers who equalize pressure in the middle ears during descent may experience vertigo during ascent. Blockage in a eustachian tube, such as a mucus plug, may prevent high-pressure air in one middle ear from escaping during ascent. When the blockage dislodges quickly, the sudden drop in air pressure in the middle ear causes immediate disorientation called alternobaric (changing pressure) vertigo.

A common method to equalize pressure in the ears is the Valsalva maneuver, which involves attempting to exhale against a closed mouth and sealed nostrils. Using excessive force during a Valsalva maneuver can cause the round window in the inner ear (see figure 4.15) to rupture. A round window rupture does not cause vertigo, but does cause permanent hearing loss.

Disorientation, the principal problem resulting from aquatic ear injuries, impairs a victim's ability to discern up and down. There are documented cases of panicked scuba divers swimming horizontally in an effort to reach the surface. Disoriented divers need a fixed point of reference, and that may be difficult to obtain in a weightless environment. A rock, anchor line, or a buddy can provide a reference until a victim's equilibrium returns. The buddy system encouraged for swimming and scuba diving certainly has merit when a person experiences disorientation while immersed or submerged. Swimmers and scuba divers who lose consciousness and sink to the bottom suffer ear injuries because they are unable to equalize the pressure in their ears.

Sinus Injuries

The same problem that causes ear injuries—unequal internal and external pressures—can also injure sinuses (see figure 4.16). Healthy sinuses equalize pressure

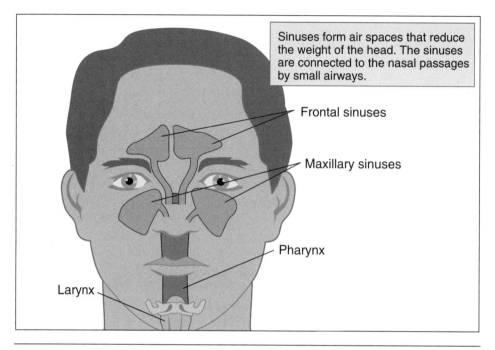

Figure 4.16 Sinuses must not be congested when subjected to water pressure.
Adapted, by permission, from D.K. Graver, 2003, *Scuba Diving*, 3rd edition (Champaign, IL: Human Kinetics), 97.

automatically, but congested sinus passages can prevent equalization. Scuba divers who submerge with nasal congestion are prone to sinus injuries; they should refrain from diving until their health returns to normal. Sinus injuries are painful and can be severe.

The use of decongestants to permit scuba diving during bouts of illness should be avoided. The medication may open sinus passages to allow pressure equalization during descent, but the increased pressure of oxygen at depth can cause the effects of the medicine to end prematurely. Without medication, the sinus passages close tightly while the diver is at depth. When the diver ascends, high-pressure air remains trapped inside the sinus. The damage can be extreme. One diver's sinus actually exploded during ascent.

Avoiding pressure at depth when congested is the key to preventing sinus injuries. Do not submerge when you have a respiratory ailment, and do not attempt to use medications for the relief of illness-related congestion to permit scuba diving.

Response

Loss of consciousness is an obvious sign of distress, but less severe problems involving the heart, brain, lungs, ears, or neurological system may require investigation. Be suspect of any person in the water who does not respond to questions. Confusion, disorientation, breathing difficulty, and incapacitation are serious signs. For conscious victims, provide reassurance and extricate them from the water as quickly as possible. Do not allow a person who does not appear normal to exert themselves in an attempt to exit the water. The effort could be the final straw and cause total collapse.

If a seizure occurs in the water at the surface, you must do your best to keep the victim's mouth and nose above water. The throat will be locked shut, so you should not attempt rescue breathing until the seizure subsides. Rescue procedures for a submerged victim who experiences a seizure are included in chapter 7.

First Aid

Heart, brain, lung, and neurological injuries are among the most life-threatening conditions that a victim can experience. Obtaining medical aid, maintaining an open and clear airway, ensuring breathing or doing rescue breathing, and ensuring circulation or providing manual circulation are the top priorities. Loosen restrictive clothing. If the victim is experiencing breathing difficulty, keep the person's head and shoulders raised to facilitate breathing.

Keep the victim's airway clear. Do all that you can to prevent aspiration of fluids. Roll the victim to the side to drain the mouth and throat when you detect gurgling sounds. Include manual suction devices in your first aid equipment for aquatic emergencies.

Citizens usually do not administer medications, but when a victim has a known condition that has reached a critical stage and medical aid will be delayed or unavailable, rescuers may assist the victim with prescribed medication. Examples include nitroglycerin for chest pain, glucose for diabetic victims (who are able to swallow), inhalers for breathing disorders, and epinephrine injectors for allergic reactions. People who require such medications should make others aware of the need for the medicine and provide advance instructions concerning administration.

A conscious person experiencing a possible heart attack should be allowed to assume a position of comfort, which will be sitting. Forcing the victim to lie down will increase breathing difficulty. Sweating, nausea, and vomiting are common. People with chest pain may be allowed to take an aspirin provided they are not taking any prescription blood-thinning medications.

A conscious person experiencing a possible brain attack should be placed in a horizontal position on the left side. The victim's head should be elevated slightly. Monitor the victim closely and continuously.

A victim of convulsive seizures should not be restrained, and nothing should be placed in the person's mouth. Place padding beneath the back of the head of the victim, who should be horizontal. As the convulsions subside, roll the victim to the left side to drain accumulated saliva from the airway. Check breathing and circulation.

Anyone with signs and symptoms of heart, lung, or brain injury will benefit from oxygen first aid. There are oxygen first aid classes for scuba divers and for lifeguards, but anyone who wants to learn the techniques may take the course and benefit from the training. Oxygen is extremely beneficial for victims of submersion injuries. People engaging in aquatic activities in remote areas should consider having an oxygen delivery system and obtaining training to use it.

Victims who experience ear or sinus injuries need to see an ear doctor as soon as possible. Waiting to see if an ear condition improves may result in severe and permanent hearing loss that could have been avoided with prompt treatment.

Prevention

The prevention of cardiovascular emergencies is the mission of the American Heart Association. People can take many actions to reduce the chances of having a heart attack or stroke. The goal of this section is to prevent such disasters from occurring while a person is in water.

The first step is to ensure that your heart, circulatory system, and lungs are normal before participating in aquatic sports in which you are submerged. A good physical examination by a licensed physician is a good place to start. Consult with the physician about your plans, especially if you are about to make a sudden change in your physical activity level.

Have your blood pressure and cholesterol levels checked regularly and keep both within recommended limits. Exercise several times weekly. The more closely your daily exercise approximates your weekend and vacation aquatic activities, the better. Bowling will not benefit the surfer, and golf will not benefit the scuba diver. Swimming would be of benefit for both of these aquatic endeavors.

A healthy lifestyle contributes greatly to the reduction of cardiovascular problems. Avoid the use of alcohol, tobacco, and drugs, and learn to manage stress. Statistics show that the State of Utah, with a large population of members of the Church of Jesus Christ of Latter-Day Saints, has far fewer deaths from heart attack and stroke than nearly all other states. The Latter-Day Saints abstain from all substances that are harmful to the body and benefit with longer, healthier lives. You can do the same by avoiding harmful habits.

If you have a history of circulatory or pulmonary medical problems, avoid in-the-water aquatic activities and use extra precautions, such as flotation devices and insulating garments, when in or around the water. Restrict boating activities to large, stable vessels that are not likely to capsize or sink, and avoid aquatic locations that are far from medical facilities.

People with normal health who desire to take up scuba diving should obtain a physical examination from a physician qualified in dive medicine. Tests are available that indicate that a person may be at risk for heart rhythm irregularities caused by immersion. Dr. McDonough et al. (1989) discovered that breath-hold facial immersion tests could detect cardiac rhythm abnormalities. The doctors of the Department of Cardiology at St. Thomas' Hospital in London found that cold stimulation combined with breathing higher-than-normal concentrations of oxygen (which scuba divers do) can create an abnormal increase in blood pressure in otherwise healthy individuals (Wilmshurst et al. 1989). Blood tests can detect abnormally high red blood cell counts, which increase the risk of cardiovascular events because clotting is more likely.

People age 40 and over should consider noninvasive testing to detect potential cardiovascular problems. Ultrasonic testing can detect diseased arteries. Identification of these problems can allow potential victims to avert a heart attack or a stroke. The miracle of modern technology offers CAT scans, MRIs, and other specialized tests to obtain internal images of the body. Ultrasonic testing is moderately expensive and imaging tests are expensive, but the price that you pay for failing to identify a problem could be infinite.

Even the healthy young athlete should take steps to avoid cardiovascular problems that could occur in aquatic settings. Avoiding dehydration and excessive heat loss are good practices. Avoiding situations in which a combination of factors could put you over the edge is another wise action. A sleep-deprived, fatigued, cold, stressed, undernourished individual who drank too much the night before could become a victim. Use common sense. Aquatic endeavors can be strenuous and stressful. Be as physically and mentally fit as possible before you participate.

Follow all recommendations to avoid ear, sinus, and venomous marine life injuries. The primary purpose of scuba diving instruction is to teach participants how to prevent and avoid injuries. Scuba diving can be a safe and highly enjoyable activity for those who abide by safe diving practices.

Finally, if you have a history of heart, lung, or brain problems, I strongly recommend that you avoid or limit some aquatic activities even if your family physician grants permission. Scuba diving in cold water, for example, may not be a good idea for a person with marginal health. The risks for some individuals engaging in scuba activities are simply far greater than the benefits. On the other hand, scuba diving in warm, calm water may be a safe and enjoyable pastime for someone whose physical condition is good, but not perfect.

Key Points

Risks are associated with any activity. Some risks are reasonable, and some are unreasonable. People who do not have health problems take a reasonable risk when they participate in aquatic activities, but people with health problems take an unreasonable risk. Be extremely cautious about water-related activities if you have health concerns, especially those related to the heart, the lungs, and the brain.

Chapter 5

Spinal Cord Injuries

It is completely devastating to be normal and healthy one second and completely helpless the next. This is the consequence of spinal cord injury. The University of Alabama at Burlington reports more than 10,000 spinal cord victims annually. Sports injuries, including headfirst diving, account for slightly more than 7 percent of the statistics. Decompression illness caused by scuba diving accidents is another cause of spinal cord damage in aquatics. We will address these and other causes in this chapter.

A HANDSOME YOUNG SCUBA DIVING CHARTER BOAT CAPTAIN in California seemed to have everything going his way until the day that he made repetitive dives to 160 feet to catch lobster. Following the second dive, he developed signs and symptoms of severe decompression sickness. After years of rehabilitation and wheelchair confinement, he finally is able to walk awkwardly with the aid of crutches. He violated the time limits for extreme depth and paid the price when excess nitrogen dissolved in his blood and tissues and formed bubbles in his spinal cord. Ascending too quickly and lowering the pressure too fast causes the excess gas to form bubbles in the tissues and blood the same way that bubbles form in soda when the can is opened suddenly and the pressure drops. Limiting time at depth, ascending slowly, and stopping during ascent can prevent decompression illness. This diver ignored the rules of safe diving and paid the price.

A **15-YEAR-OLD BOY AND HIS FRIEND** were playing golf at a housing community in Wisconsin on a beautiful summer day. After playing golf and consuming a couple of beers, the two decided to cool off in the community lake. The soon-to-be victim knew that the lake was only two feet deep, but he ran the length of the dock and dived headfirst into the water. He floated to the surface and did not move. His friend jumped into the water and carefully turned him over. The victim said that he was unable to move. The friend called for help, sent a bystander to phone 911, and supported the victim in the warm water until medical personnel arrived. The victim was immobilized, removed from the water, and taken to a medical facility. After a year of medical care and therapy, the boy made a complete recovery. He is one of the fortunate few whose lapse of common sense did not confine him to a wheelchair for life.

Learning Goals *By the end of this chapter, you should be able to:*

- ▶ State three causes of aquatic spinal cord injuries and the spinal area most often affected by these injuries.
- ▶ List three types of disability that may result from spinal cord injury.
- ▶ Describe the neutral alignment position for the cervical spine.
- ▶ Describe the modified jaw-thrust technique for opening the airway of an unconscious victim who may have a spinal cord injury.
- ▶ Explain how to assess a conscious victim for spinal cord injury.
- ▶ Describe two ways to immobilize a victim with a possible spinal injury who is immersed in water.
- ▶ Describe three ways to extricate a victim with a possible spinal injury who is immersed in water.
- ▶ Explain the procedure for a deep-water backboard extrication onto a boat or dock.
- ▶ List three first aid procedures for spinal cord injuries.
- ▶ List 10 of 13 recommendations to avoid spinal cord injuries.

Causes

Children's Hospital and Medical Center (1992) in Seattle, Washington, reports that nationwide there are as many as 700 headfirst diving-related spinal cord injuries each year. The Divers Alert Network (2001) reports that 274 of the 431 divers who were injured in 1998 had neurological symptoms. In addition to headfirst diving and scuba diving, spinal cord injuries—especially those to the cervical spine in the neck—result from head injuries. Water skiers who are struck in the head by a watercraft are likely to have an injury to the cervical spine. Boaters and water skiers who are thrown into the water at high speeds can sustain neck injuries. When a swimmer jumps into the water onto another swimmer, a spinal cord injury can occur. Surfing and surfboards can injure the neck and back. The Spinal Cord Injury Information Network (2001) reports 11,000 spinal cord injuries per year. Fifty-one percent of the accidents occur to victims between 15 and 35 years of age with 82 percent of those injured being male (King County EMS 2000).

Jumping into shallow water can cause spinal injuries (see figure 5.1). If the water level is not at least chest deep, impact with the bottom can be strong enough to injure the spinal column. The greater the height of the jump, the greater the potential for injury. Even if the water is deep, the impact of jumping onto a submerged object, such as a tree, can transfer enough energy to the spine to cause severe damage.

CC Lockwood/Bruce Coleman Inc.

Figure 5.1 Jumping or diving into shallow water can cause injury and should not be allowed.

Anatomy and Physiology

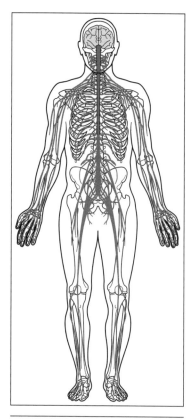

Figure 5.2 The nervous system consists of the brain and spinal cord (central nervous system) and the nerves that branch from the spinal cord to all parts of the body (peripheral nervous system). Damage to the brain or spine can cause permanent damage to the nervous system.

The brain and spinal cord comprise the central nervous system (CNS) (see figure 5.2). The spinal cord derives some protection by being encased inside 33 vertebrae, which are stacked on top of each other to form the spinal column. The first seven bones of the top of the spine are the cervical vertebrae. Approximately 55 percent of all spinal injuries occur in the cervical region (King County EMS 2000).

The brain sends and receives signals via the spinal cord. Both motor and sensory nerves from the spinal cord branch out between the vertebrae and extend to every part of the body. Motor nerves control movement and sensory nerves provide stimulus information such as pain or temperature. Injury can exert pressure on nerves, which can cause temporary impairment, or may sever nerves, which can cause permanent neurological disability.

The higher in the spine that an injury occurs, the more serious the consequences will be. A severe injury to the first few cervical vertebrae can cause respiratory arrest because the nerves to the diaphragm may be damaged (Mistovich et al. 2000, 660-661). Cervical spinal injuries may result in paralysis of all four extremities and the trunk (quadriplegia). Severe spinal cord injuries that occur lower in the spinal cord may cause paralysis of the lower extremities (paraplegia) and bowel and bladder dysfunction. Less severe injuries may cause burning, tingling, numbness, or weakness in the extremities.

Recognition

Spinal cord injury must be assumed until it can be ruled out. Suspect spinal cord injury for any high-energy accident or when a victim has a head injury. Immediately immobilize the head in a neutral position—eyes aimed straight ahead and perpendicular to the spine. Rotating the victim's head is acceptable as long as there is no resistance to movement. A neutral position places the least amount of pressure on the nerve bundles inside the vertebrae.

An adult lying on the back requires about one-half to three-quarters of an inch of padding beneath the head to maintain neutral alignment. A child or infant may require padding beneath the shoulders for neutral alignment because the head may be large in proportion to the body. Do not lift a child or infant's body to insert padding. Use several people to log-roll the victim (keep the head, neck, and spine in a straight line) onto one side, place the padding, and then roll the victim back onto the padding.

Whenever possible, dedicate one rescuer to immobilizing the victim's head while you perform a simple neurological assessment. If you are alone, do your best to do both tasks. If the victim is not breathing, use the modified jaw-thrust method to maintain the airway for rescue breathing (see figure 5.3).

Rapidly assess a victim's neurological status by asking if he has any neck or back pain and how his extremities feel. Ask if he has any unusual sensations in the extremities. Ask him to wiggle his fingers and toes. If the extremities feel normal and move normally, spinal cord injury is not likely. If an accident is significant, however—such as a fall from a substantial height—keep the person still and maintain spinal immobilization until he has been evaluated by medical personnel. A secondary injury may result from swelling, loss of circulation, or

Figure 5.3 When you suspect a spinal injury, use a modified jaw thrust to open the airway by lifting the jaw without tilting the head.

movement of bone fragments. If the victim has a neurological injury, evaluate the affected areas. Test strength by having the victim push both feet against hand resistance at the same time and by having the victim squeeze both of your hands simultaneously. If he is experiencing numbness, determine how far up the body the numbness extends. If he is experiencing burning or tingling, determine the exact areas affected. If you are alone, conduct your testing verbally while you immobilize the spine. When you have someone to maintain cervical-spinal immobilization, do a physical and a verbal examination.

Response

The four parts of a rescue for a victim with a suspected spinal injury are as follows:

1. Immobilization
2. Righting a victim who is in a face-down position
3. Airway and breathing management
4. Extrication from the water

We will examine each step separately. Keep in mind that rescue procedures are merely guidelines and that you may need to improvise while keeping basic principles in mind. As long as you cause no further harm to the victim, it doesn't matter what method you use to immobilize or extricate the person.

Immobilization

Since rescue situations vary greatly, so must rescue techniques. At times you just have to do your best to immobilize the victim and hope for the best. The water may be shallow or deep, calm or rough, cold or warm. The victim may be conscious or unconscious, breathing or not breathing, face up or face down, and wearing anything from swimming trunks to a full exposure suit. The following immobilization methods can help keep the head, neck, and spine aligned to prevent further injury to the spinal cord.

Cradling the victim's head by positioning it between the victim's arms extended beside the head as shown in figure 5.4 is a simple immobilization method that works well for most rescue situations. Place one of your arms behind the victim's head and the other beneath the victim's back to support the trunk of the body. Pull the sandwich of the victim's arms and head against your chest and maintain a constant pressure to prevent the victim's head from moving.

Righting a Victim

A victim found in a face-down position may be inverted using the head cradle inversion technique just described. Extend the victim's arms beside the head and use them to hold the head. Use one hand to pull the victim against your body and place the other hand on the victim's arm that is against your body.

a

b

Figure 5.4 *(a)* Sandwich the victim's head between his arms and keep pressure on the arms while rolling him to a face-up position. *(b)* Maintain pressure on the victim's arms while supporting him with the rescue float.

Roll the victim toward you while squeezing the victim's head between the arms constantly and exchange the positions of your hands. When the victim is face up, reposition your hands one at a time to support the back of the victim's head and the trunk of the body. The steps of this tricky, but effective, maneuver are shown in figure 5.4.

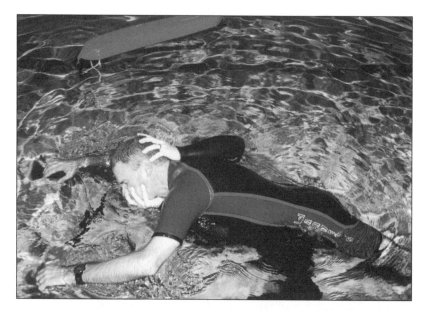

a

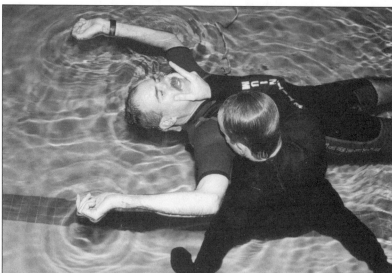

b

Figure 5.5 Forearms splinting technique. *(a)* Keep the victim's head in a neutral position by sandwiching the victim with your forearms along the breastbone and spine. Cover the victim's mouth and nose with your hand, position your head in front of the victim's shoulder, and roll the victim to an upright position. *(b)* When you surface on the opposite side of the victim, bridge your hand and fingers to allow the victim to breathe and maintain pressure on your forearms to support the head, neck, and back in a neutral position.

When the victim initially is in a face-down position and you suspect a spinal injury, the forearms splinting technique depicted in figure 5.5 is a good technique. The method works well once mastered, but some students have difficulty grasping the skill concept. Practicing with coaching by a water rescue instructor familiar with the technique will develop your ability to use this valuable procedure. The primary idea of this technique is to support the head, neck, and back using one forearm aligned with the breastbone and the other forearm aligned with the spine and holding the victim in alignment by pressing the forearms together constantly. This method requires the rescuer to lean to the side. The hand of the arm on the front of the victim seals the victim's mouth and nose initially and then slides to a bridge position after the victim's face is above water. Turning the victim from a face-down to a face-up position while using the forearm splinting technique works well, but the technique requires practice. You must position your head beneath the victim and in front of the victim's chest. As you duck beneath the victim, roll the victim to a face-up position while maintaining spinal immobilization. You will end up on the opposite side of the victim as shown in figure 5.5.

When the victim is wearing clothing and the water is calm, less effort will be required to maintain spinal immobilization if you use the technique shown in figure 5.6. Assume a position in front of the victim (at the head), grasp the victim's clothing at the shoulders, and immobilize the victim's head and neck with constant pressure exerted inward with your forearms.

Figure 5.6 You may use your forearms to support a victim's head when the water is shallow and calm and the victim is buoyant.

Airway and Breathing Management

When the victim is not breathing, you will need to combine first aid with a rescue. Aquatic rescue breathing is difficult, but definitely possible. The use of a rescue breathing mask is recommended, especially if the victim may have a spinal cord injury. The head-tilt, chin-lift method of opening the airway cannot be used for obvious reasons. Mouth-to-mouth rescue breathing is an extremely difficult maneuver without a breathing mask on land and even more difficult in the water. Mouth-to-mask breathing works on land, in the water, and with the head-tilt, the chin-lift, or the jaw-thrust technique (see figure 5.7).

Figure 5.7 A rescue breathing mask and a jaw-thrust airway maneuver are the best techniques for aquatic rescue breathing when you suspect a spinal cord injury and the victim is not breathing.

Extrication

With the victim's spine immobilized manually and breathing assured, the next task is to remove the victim from the water without causing additional harm to the spinal cord. Factors to consider at this point include the following:

- Water temperature
- Water conditions
- Water depth
- Number of rescuers

- Rescuer training
- Immobilization devices available
- Approximate time for professional rescuers to arrive
- Victim's condition

Taking all factors into consideration, you must decide whether it is best to remove a victim with a possible spinal cord injury from the water or to keep the immobilized victim in the water until professional help arrives. If the water is calm and warm and the victim's condition is good, the latter is the best choice. But if the water is cold and the victim's condition is poor, the victim must be extricated expeditiously using the best means available to keep the spine immobilized. If you must extricate a victim with a spinal injury before professional help arrives or when professional help is not available, the following methods can work effectively if you have learned them in advance and have practiced them.

The hammock carry is a simple, effective extrication technique that does not require any equipment. One trained rescuer who recruits and instructs two bystanders can remove a victim from shallow water using this method (see figure 5.8). The rescuer supports the victim in the cradle position, one assistant rescuer supports the victim's lower back and buttocks on the opposite side, and a second assistant rescuer supports the victim's legs on the same side as the trained

Figure 5.8 While not the best method, a hammock carry is an acceptable improvised extrication method for an injured victim.

rescuer. With practice, the victim can be lifted from the water and carried to shore without bending or twisting the spine. Once ashore, a fourth person can be recruited to hold the victim's arms tightly together while the three carriers lower the victim to the ground and carefully remove their arms from beneath the victim. If a fourth person is not available, the three carriers lower the victim to the ground and the two holding the head and back continue to support the victim. Meanwhile, the assistant who was carrying the legs moves to the head and holds the victim's arms tightly together to support the head while the remaining two carriers carefully remove their arms from beneath the victim.

When the water is deep initially and the distance to shallow water and shore is not great, the rescuer can keep the victim immobilized using the arm cradle technique, swim the victim to shallow water, and have bystanders assist with the hammock carry to extricate the victim. By moving slowly backward and shuffling the feet, you can carry a victim from the water without removing your swim fins. Practice is required to avoid tripping and falling. When extra help is available, have a bystander remove your fins before carrying the victim from the water.

At a shallow, sloping beach where there are no bystanders to assist, a single rescuer can extricate a victim with a possible spinal cord injury using a horsecollar drag. Take a blanket by one corner and quickly spin it to form a long, narrow sash. While floating the victim in calm water, place the center of the sash at the back of the victim's neck. Bring both ends around the neck, cross them, pass them beneath the arms and back up the neck. Grasp the blanket ends, and the shoulder loops created by the blanket, and carefully drag the victim from the water, keeping the person as level as possible to avoid putting pressure on the spine. Figure 5.9 shows an alternate extrication technique.

Figure 5.9 A single-rescuer extrication technique using a blanket or rescue strap to drag a victim to shore on a shallow, sloping beach.

Lifeguards at swimming pools have backboards for the immobilization of victims with possible spinal cord injuries and are trained in the procedures to secure a victim to the backboard and remove the victim from the water (see figure 5.10). People who are likely to face this type of emergency, such as a family who has a cabin on a lake where many friends come to swim and play, should consider taking lifeguard training and having basic rescue equipment at the site where an aquatic emergency is likely to occur. Practicing immobilization and extrication techniques for simulated spinal injuries several times each year will keep family members prepared to deal with this type of emergency and will serve as a reminder to use caution when swimming and playing in and around water.

Figure 5.10 Backboard immobilization is the ideal extrication method for victims with suspected spinal injuries.

THE TECHNIQUES FOR AQUATIC SPINAL IMMOBILIZATION described thus far leave much to be desired when the water is rough, cold, and deep. Even conventional aquatic backboarding methods compromise the victim's spine because the process is slow and there is too much movement. Boeing water rescue personnel assisted with a water rescue course that I taught for the fire department in Renton, Washington. I noticed some peculiar head blocks on their backboard and asked about them. The procedure they use to extricate a victim with a possible spinal cord injury is to push the backboard beneath the victim and float it into place so the victim's head is positioned between the head blocks. The Boeing rescuers then quickly secure the victim to the board and pull the backboard onto the rescue vessel. The rescuers do not attempt to secure the victim's head while in the water. The blocks minimize movement. I have practiced the technique and now include it when I train marine rescue units for fire departments.

There is a trick to getting a victim secured to a backboard onto a boat in deep water. In my water rescue classes, we use two rescuers aboard the boat and two rescue swimmers in the water. The rescue swimmers position torpedo buoys beneath the backboard to push it up against the victim. The backboard is positioned perpendicular to the boat and the rescuers aboard the vessel each hold one corner of the head of the board. The rescue swimmers remove the torpedo buoys while supporting the foot of the backboard. The swimmers clip the ends of the buoys together to form donuts and place one leg through the circle. By riding the buoy donut, extending their arms, and swimming hard with fins, two rescuer swimmers can keep a backboard nearly level while the two rescuers aboard the boat lift the other end of the backboard and pull it across the gunwale and onto the vessel (see figure 5.11). The lift and pull must

Figure 5.11 Two rescuers aboard a boat and two rescuers in the water can keep a backboarded victim nearly level during extrication.

be coordinated because the rescue swimmers are able to hold up the foot of the board for only a few seconds. This procedure requires practice and coordination to be effective.

First Aid

There are three important aspects of first aid for spinal cord injuries. As previously covered, the most important actions are immobilization, righting the victim, ensuring adequate breathing, and extricating the victim. Another important priority is treating the victim for shock, which can be profound for victims of spinal cord injuries. Signs of shock include anxiety, paleness, nausea, rapid breathing, and rapid pulse. Make sure that the victim is dry and warm. If possible, administer oxygen. See additional first aid procedures for shock in chapter 9.

Prevention

Dive into water only in areas designated for diving. A designated diving area must meet the following criteria:

- Depth at least 10 feet for diving from the edge
- Depth at least 12 feet if diving from a diving board
- Opposite wall at least 25 feet from the point where a dive will be completed

In addition, divers should adhere to the following rules:

- Dive only from the front end of a diving board.
- Avoid attempting difficult dives without qualified instruction.
- Avoid competition dives in residential swimming pools.
- Avoid drinking alcohol and diving.
- Avoid diving from any platform not designed for diving.
- Adhere to all recommended scuba diving safety practices.
- Avoid jumping into unfamiliar water.
- Jump into water only when it is at least chest deep.
- Grip toes on the edge when jumping so you will push away from the side.
- Avoid jumping backward from a pool edge.

Key Points

Spinal cord injuries or even suspected injuries pose significant problems for water rescuers. The most important priority is maintaining the head in neutral alignment to minimize pressure on the spinal cord. Breathing is the second concern. If the victim is not breathing, a jaw-thrust maneuver must be used to open the airway without tilting the head back. After the victim is stabilized, rescue exits must be done in a manner that will maintain the spinal column in a straight line. Various factors, including water conditions and temperature, affect a rescuer's decision to remove the victim from the water or to support the victim in the water until medical personnel arrive. After a victim has been removed from the water, treatment for shock is an important consideration.

Part III

Water Sports

Chapter **6**

Swimming Injuries

Swimming is the most popular recreational activity; both swimmers and nonswimmers "go swimming." Submersion injuries are not limited to non-swimmers. Many good swimmers drown for a variety of reasons. The purpose of this chapter is to explain the causes of swimming accidents to help informed individuals avoid the potential consequences.

In addition to water movement and heat loss, swimming accidents result from blackouts, cramping, head injuries, and more. In this chapter you will learn about various problems that affect swimmers and how to prevent them.

DURING THE 1980s, a woman swimming in the ocean in California felt herself being pushed out to sea. She swam vigorously toward shore, but made no progress. Exhausted, she called for help. Her husband on the beach heard her and went to her aid. He had no difficulty reaching her, but was unable to get her back to shore. The wife panicked, clutched and incapacitated her husband, and both of them drowned. This is a tragic accident that could have been prevented if either the woman or her husband had known about rip currents.

AN OBESE MAN RENTED AN ALUMINUM SKIFF and went on a solo ocean excursion near Santa Barbara, California. He anchored the vessel and enjoyed the solitude. It was a warm day, so he decided to go for a swim. He entered the cool water and swam near the boat. A few minutes later he returned to the vessel, but was unable to get aboard. He was forced to hang onto the side of the boat and wait for help. Several friends and I were returning from a scuba diving outing when we noticed the man clinging to the side of the vessel. We stopped, inquired, and learned of his plight. It took all of us to lift the poor chap into his boat. He became incapacitated. We towed his boat to shore and called emergency medical personnel, who transported the man to the hospital. He was suffering from severe hypothermia.

Learning Goals *By the end of this chapter, you should be able to:*

- Define hyperventilation and explain how it can cause a person to lose consciousness underwater.
- List three recommendations to avoid loss of consciousness while immersed.
- State the greatest single contributor to submersion injuries.
- List three factors that affect how ocean waves break on shore.
- Describe how a rip current is formed, how to recognize one, and how to escape from the current.
- Describe the proper attire for immersion into swift-flowing water.
- Explain what to do if you are plunged suddenly into swift-flowing water.
- Explain a major hazard associated with canals.
- Define a cramp, list three causes of cramps, explain how to minimize cramps, and explain how to relieve a cramp while immersed.
- Explain why people can be injured when they breathe compressed air at depth and then ascend.
- List five reasons adolescent swimmers are likely to experience a submersion injury.
- State the best method to prevent children from experiencing a submersion injury.
- List five of six questions to ask bystanders while assessing an aquatic rescue situation.
- Describe two ways to throw a rescue rope.

▶ Explain the value of a tether line for rescuers and explain the procedures for using one.

▶ Describe three types of assists for swimmers in distress.

▶ Explain three ways to use floats for deep-water rescues.

▶ Explain how to do mouth-to-mask rescue breathing in deep water.

Blackouts

A blackout in or under water will cause drowning. Individuals who experience loss of consciousness should avoid immersion. Healthy people with no history of blackouts, however, can also experience loss of consciousness with its consequences.

Breath-hold swimming and skin diving deaths are often the result of participants losing consciousness underwater. Breath holders swim horizontally while holding their breath, and skin divers swim vertically and horizontally while holding their breath. The problem, which is greater for skin divers, stems from deep and rapid breathing (hyperventilation) in advance of the breath holding (see figure 6.1). The body's primary stimulus for breathing is an increase in the carbon dioxide level in the blood. Carbon dioxide is the by-product of metabolism. Hyperventilation lowers carbon dioxide in the body and extends the length of time required for the gas to increase to the point at which there is an urge to breathe. The body is able to use more of the oxygen in air when underwater, but the oxygen level decreases during ascent. The combination of delayed response to breathing stimulus and the rapid drop in oxygen during ascent can cause blackouts without warning. Exertion while breath holding after hyperventilation hastens loss of consciousness. Many blackouts occur when people attempt extended time periods underwater while holding their breath.

THE FIT YOUNG MAN WAS A CANDIDATE in a scuba diving instructor course in Chicago in 1975. To qualify as an instructor, he had to swim 75 feet underwater with no push off or dive. This was a difficult task for him, but he was determined to succeed. He ducked beneath the surface of the swimming pool and started swimming to the other end. About 10 feet from the deep end of the pool, his motions became erratic, and then he went limp. One of my staff members dived into the water and brought the victim to the surface. We pulled him from the pool, placed him on the deck, opened his airway, and checked for breathing. Much to our relief, he was breathing. Moments later he regained consciousness. He had hyperventilated and blacked out as a consequence. After a medical evaluation at a local hospital, the candidate was able to continue his training.

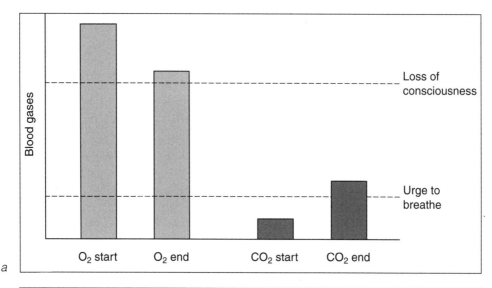

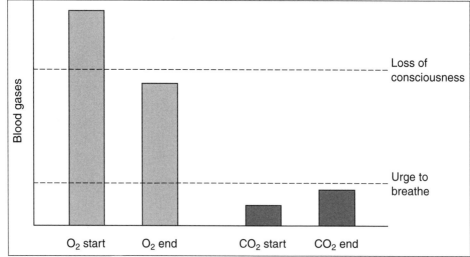

Figure 6.1 *(a)* Breath holding without hyperventilation. *(b)* Breath holding after hyperventilation. Excessive hyperventilation can lead to loss of consciousness underwater because oxygen levels decrease too much before there is an adequate stimulus to breathe.

Avoidance of this serious problem is simple—avoid hyperventilation prior to breath holding underwater. Limit deep breaths to three, which will lower carbon dioxide slightly to increase breath-hold time, but not enough to create a condition that can cause loss of consciousness.

Hyperventilation is not the only cause of blackouts. I know of several situations in which a combination of factors caused loss of consciousness. Lean individuals who do not eat, become cold, and exercise strenuously may lose consciousness from low blood sugar. Good nutrition a couple of hours before participating in aquatic activities can prevent the problem.

Even healthy swimmers who eat right and do not hyperventilate can lose consciousness from a blow to the head. A tragic cause of drowning is hitting the head on swimming pool sides and bottoms, submerged rocks and logs, and overhead obstructions while ascending. Boats, jet skis, and other watercraft may strike a swimmer in the head. Kayakers are well aware of the problem; helmets are standard equipment for them. Swimmers do not need to wear helmets, but they must be careful to avoid hitting their heads.

Following a few simple rules can prevent a blow to the head that can cause loss of consciousness and drowning. Avoid diving into murky water in rivers, ponds, and other bodies of water. Scuba divers should avoid diving when the water movement is strong and the visibility is poor. More than one scuba diver has died from drowning caused by a blow to the head in rough water. Avoid headfirst dives into shallow swimming pools. Never dive into above ground swimming pools. Look at the wall of a swimming pool as you approach it. If you dive into a clear, deep pool, be sure that the opposite wall is at least 25 feet away. Keep your hands extended above your head when swimming underwater and ascending. Never swim alone; having another swimmer present can save your life if you do lose consciousness.

Heat Loss

Let's apply the problems of hypothermia addressed in chapter 3 to swimmers. When body temperature decreases, judgment and memory are affected. People who know that they need to exit the water when they are cold are likely to forget what they know. I have advised people who have lost body heat to the point at which they have stopped shivering to stay out of the water and am always amazed when they tell me that they're fine. A common statement is, "It's OK. I'm used to the water now." I know that they know better, but heat loss has robbed them of their reasoning. Additional exposure at that point leads quickly to significant problems that include cramping, muscle stiffness and rigidity, and loss of swimming ability. The best swimmer can drown without flotation when hypothermia occurs. The colder the water is, the faster this scenario occurs.

REMEMBER THE STORY FROM CHAPTER 3 about the yacht club member in Everett, Washington, that fell overboard during a race. He survived, but was quite disturbed by his experience. When I explained the physiological process of hypothermia, the man who had fallen overboard exclaimed, "That's exactly what happened to me. After about 10 minutes I could barely move my legs."

Perhaps the single most common contributor to submersion injuries is the consumption of alcohol, which is a factor in half of all water accidents. The primary reason for this is that alcohol increases the loss of body heat. Alcohol ingestion causes blood vessels near the skin to dilate, bringing warm blood closer to the surface of the body. Heat loss increases substantially. Contrary to the myth that alcoholic drinks provide warmth, they can rapidly lead to profound hypothermia, especially in water. In addition, alcohol also impairs judgment and decreases a person's ability to shiver. Aquatic pursuits require you to be in the best mental and physical condition possible. Inhibiting yourself with alcohol can be the cause of your death. Avoid alcohol when in or around water.

Water Movement

Wind, tides, the earth's rotation, and gravity all cause water to move. Surf, currents, and swift water can pose hazards to swimmers, especially when they are unexpected or when the victim is uninformed. Deaths occur every year because people fall into rivers and canals, get tumbled by waves, and fight against ocean currents until exhausted. Those who venture into water must develop a profound respect for its power. Water is 800 times denser than air and weighs over eight pounds per gallon. If you try to fight water in motion, you will lose. Your only chance is to use it to your advantage.

The Ocean

Wind forms waves in water. A wave is energy traveling through water with little movement of the water itself until the wave breaks on a distant shore. When the wave breaks, it releases its stored energy. The stronger and longer the wind blows in one direction, the larger the resulting waves will be. Large waves are incredibly powerful and can break with crushing force. Waves can bend in shallow water and can reflect from vertical surfaces, such as a seawall. Waves break in different ways depending on the slope and type of bottom. On some steep, sandy beaches, waves approaching at an angle cause water to flow along the shore (see figure 6.2). The flow of water cuts a trench a few feet from shore. Unsuspecting people wading into the water may panic or perish when they encounter the dropoff. When waves break over an offshore sandbar, they can pile water up on the shore and create a powerful rip current when a channel running from the shore is formed by the return flow of the excess water. Before playing in the ocean, you need to know the environment. Swim at designated beaches staffed by lifeguards. Ask questions when you are new to an area. Do not assume that all ocean beaches are similar.

AFTER SKIN DIVING AND SCUBA DIVING IN SANTA BARBARA, California, for a few years, I went to a beach near Los Angeles in pursuit of Pismo clams. The ocean looked calm. The waves were breaking right next to shore, and I noticed that they broke all at once. I was used to spilling breakers that broke offshore and rolled all the way to the beach. When I entered the water, I waited until a wave broke, ran in, and swam beyond the area where the waves broke before the next wave arrived—no problem. I had an inner tube with a burlap sack suspended from the center to hold the clams that I intended to find. My quest was successful. I found the clams just where I had been told to look, and I soon had my limit. My standard practice in Santa Barbara was to place my torso on top of my inner tube and swim to shore at the end of a dive. While swimming in this manner back to shore at this new beach, I forgot about the shore break. When I was almost to shore, I felt myself being lifted slightly, and then I found myself looking straight down at wet sand. As I fell down the front of the wave, I clutched the inner tube desperately because I did not know what was happening. I landed on my face in the sand, nearly broke my neck, and was instantly tumbled by the moving water of the wave. When the wave receded, I scrambled to my knees. My mask was around my neck, my eyes and nose were full of sand, and I forgot that the waves break every few seconds. Before I could gather myself, I was tumbled by another wave. This time I recalled the wave pattern and crawled quickly beyond the surf zone before the next wave arrived. I was lucky. I could have been paralyzed for life. I have had the greatest respect for different types of waves ever since that experience.

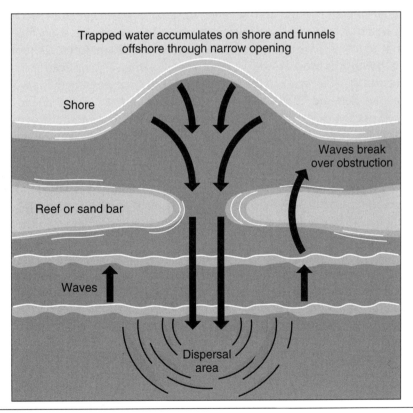

Figure 6.2 The narrow, strong current that moves away from shore is the result of water flowing back to sea through a narrow opening in an underwater obstruction.

Adapted, by permission, from D.K. Graver, 2003, *Scuba Diving,* 3rd edition (Champaign, IL: Human Kinetics), 181.

Many scuba diving accidents have occurred because divers have driven long distances to dive in the ocean only to find large waves breaking on the shore when they arrive. They make a decision to dive anyway, and their poor judgment often costs them their lives. Surfers also tend to attempt more than they should. A good rule to follow when the ocean is rough is to find an alternate location where conditions are better or to choose an alternate land-based activity until conditions improve.

Rip currents can be useful if you can recognize them and understand them. When you want to reach an offshore location, a rip current is an express ride through the surf zone. Obviously, you cannot return by the same route. You must swim parallel to shore along the beach until you are beyond the area where the water flows away from shore.

WHEN I WAS A YOUNG MAN and a candidate in a scuba instructor course in Monterey, California, my buddy, Bob, and I were participating in our first ocean training dive of the course. The instructions were simple. All we had to do was swim to a woman sitting on a paddleboard located about 250 yards from shore, tell her our names, and return to shore. There were small waves breaking almost 200 yards from shore and rolling all the way to the beach. The task did not seem difficult until we began snorkeling toward our goal. Every four seconds a wave would wash over us and push us backward a few feet. For every four feet we moved forward, we were moved back three. After 20 minutes of strenuous exertion with little progress, we were both nearly exhausted. I noticed that other candidates who had entered the water when we did were nearly to the woman on the paddleboard. They had entered farther down the beach than we did. I pointed out the divers to my partner and suggested that we move over and follow their course, and he agreed. We swam parallel with the waves for a couple of minutes and then resumed swimming away from shore. Suddenly we were making headway. We were no longer being pushed backward by the waves; in fact, the waves seemed to lack energy. Within a few minutes we were reporting to the woman on the paddleboard and making our way back to shore. We were feeling good as we walked along the beach back to the facilities when I heard a candidate in front of me say to another, "I don't think we would have made it if we had not found that rip current." Suddenly the light came on in my mind. The entire exercise was to determine if we could recognize and use a rip current. I looked back and could see the rip. I knew about rip currents from books, but had never experienced one. Ever since that gruesome, but wonderful, learning experience, I have been able to identify rip currents.

Freshwater

Freshwater can be every bit as dangerous as saltwater. Swift-flowing rivers and storm canals claim lives every year. Whitewater rafters and kayakers pit their skills against moving water. People adrift in moving water need to know what to do to avoid injury. Preparation makes a great difference. Exposure suits, personal flotation devices, helmets, tennis shoes, knowledge, training, and experience greatly increase safety.

Experienced river users know to move with the water in a feet-first position to fend off rocks and obstructions. If you find yourself in rough water, your best bet is to go with the flow, and when the water becomes calmer, slowly work your way to the nearest bank. Inexperienced victims with no equipment try to swim to shore immediately, become exhausted, get injured, become hypothermic, and often perish. Another common error is holding onto a rock or tree in the middle of a fast-moving, cold stream. The moving water increases heat loss just the way that wind increases heat loss in air, except that the effect is hundreds of times greater. You are better off drifting with cold water than staying stationary and having it flow over you. Perhaps the greatest keys to safety in any aquatic pursuit are to know the rules, have proper equipment, and avoid conditions that you are not prepared to handle.

Canals have hidden hazards. They pass beneath roads and other barriers. The water flows down through a siphon and then back up on the other side. The siphon often has a large screen, called a trash rack, to prevent debris from clogging the tunnel. People who swim in canals can be caught in the current that is produced near the siphon. The current can pull them beneath the surface and pin them against the trash rack. Canals should not be used for swimming.

Avoid drains in swimming pools. The suction from the pool circulation pump can be strong enough to trap you and cause you to drown. The U.S. Consumer Product Safety Commission (1994a) has several recommendations to prevent this hazard. The average age of victims who die from drain entrapment is 10 years old. Teach your children to stay away from drains.

Cramps

A cramp is a painful, involuntary contraction of a muscle. They usually occur when a muscle is cold and tired. The longer a muscle remains cramped, the longer it will remain sore. You need to prevent cramps, be alert for warning signs, and know how to relieve them quickly and effectively.

When I was a youth, grown-ups used to tell me to wait an hour after eating to avoid stomach cramps. That was a myth because stomach cramping is extremely rare, but the advice was good for a different reason. Eating causes a change in your circulation. About 15 percent of your blood supply diverts to your digestive tract after eating, so less circulation is available for your muscles. You want to have maximum circulation to your muscles when you swim.

Lack of minerals, especially potassium, can make muscles more prone to cramping. Eating foods rich in potassium can help prevent cramping. Stretching the muscles before exercising them also helps because it signals your body that you are going to start exerting and increases circulation to the muscles.

Inadequate circulation can also cause cramping. Tight-fitting exposure suits and footwear may restrict blood flow to muscles. Aquatic exposure suits should be snug, but not tight. Loss of body heat reduces blood flow to the extremities. Cold legs are much more likely to cramp than warm ones. Acids that accumulate in muscles that are exercised when circulation is poor also contribute to the problem. Periodic resting and pressing on tight muscles to gently push waste products from them can help prevent painful muscle contractions.

Leg and foot muscle cramps are the most common types that occur while swimming. If you are attentive to your body, you can feel tightness in muscles and twitching when a cramp is imminent. If you stop exerting and stretch the affected muscle immediately, you can prevent the muscle from cramping.

If a cramp occurs in the water in spite of all efforts to prevent one, remain calm. Find a way to stretch the affected muscle immediately (see figure 6.3). If the cramp is in your calf, hold your breath, grasp your toes with one hand, extend the cramped leg as much as possible to stretch the muscle, and use your other hand to press the muscle. Exhale into the water and lift your head periodically to quickly take a breath. Avoid pounding, squeezing, or kneading the muscle because these actions cause bruising. Pressing and rubbing are beneficial actions.

Figure 6.3   Stretch and rub a cramped muscle to release the cramp.

Compressed Air Breathing

A **YOUNG MAN WANTED TO IMPRESS HIS FRIENDS.** He tied a heavy weight to an inverted five-gallon bucket and secretly hid it under water. When his friends were present, he told them to watch how long he could hold his breath. He dived into the water, found the bucket, put his head inside it, and breathed the trapped air for several minutes. When he surfaced, he suddenly lost consciousness. He was pulled from the water and resuscitation was attempted, but his ill-advised stunt cost him his life.

Scuba divers are not the only people who can suffer lung injuries. Swimmers who breathe compressed air at depth and then ascend while breath holding can also rupture their lungs. Air in an open, inverted container is compressed by water pressure during descent. At a depth of 34 feet in freshwater or 33 feet in seawater, the volume of air in an inverted container is exactly half of what it was at the surface. When the air volume is halved, its density is doubled (Graver 1999). Breathing compressed air at depth is dangerous because the dense air will expand to its original volume during ascent. A swimmer breathing compressed air at depth—like the swimmer who breathed the air from the inverted bucket—must exhale slowly and continuously during ascent to allow expanding air to escape. Failure to exhale will cause pressure to build up in the lungs and cause them to burst.

A person inside a sinking car can experience the same problem when breathing air from an air pocket that may develop at the ceiling of the vehicle. To escape from a submerged car, wait until the water level nears the ceiling, roll down the window, exit through the open window, and swim to the surface while exhaling slowly and continuously. It is difficult or impossible to open a door unless the vehicle is completely flooded. Opening the window too soon may cause the vehicle to tip when water pours rapidly into one side.

Air that is pumped below the surface is compressed air. Always remember that breathing any form of compressed air underwater can cause a life-threatening lung injury during ascent unless you breathe out continuously to allow the expanding air to escape.

Adolescent Swimmers

Teenage and young adult swimming fatalities are, unfortunately, far too common. People at this age, especially males, like to test their bodies and exercise their independence. They consume alcohol and go swimming—a dangerous combination. They dive into unknown depths, and they jump from great heights. They may swim alone. They challenge others to swim with them to a raft, rock, or target object far from shore. The fastest swimmers race, while the less proficient fall behind. The person lagging well behind becomes tired, gives up, tries to return to shore, and perishes unnoticed by his peers until it is too late. Adolescents need to learn what causes swimming fatalities so they can avoid them.

Nonswimmers

Two-thirds of fatal aquatic accidents occur during recreation, and swimming is the most frequent recreational activity. The Royal Life Saving Society of Canada (1990) reports that the top five aquatic recreational activities in order of preference are swimming, fishing, walking near water, playing in water, and canoeing. These activities account for 82 percent of fatal recreational accidents. Individuals who want to play in water, but do not know how to swim, are at special risk and account for many aquatic fatalities. Inflatable armbands and toys are unsafe flotation devices. Consider any adult who does not know how to swim and goes boating without wearing a personal flotation device to be stupid or to have a death wish.

Constant supervision—undivided attention—is essential for children playing in water. A shocking statistic is that most children between the ages of one and three who drown were being "supervised" by one or both parents! (U.S. Consumer Product Safety Commission 1994b). In addition to being very serious about supervising their children, parents must know what to do if an accident does occur. Another statistic that causes dismay is that many children are rescued within seconds, but die because the adults who are present do not know how to do CPR or rescue breathing. Everyone age 12 and older should be able to save a life with CPR.

The majority of children under age four who drown do so at home. Home swimming pools, ponds, streams, fountains, spas, bathtubs, toilets, and even buckets are common fatality sites. Parents need to restrict access to water in and around their homes and supervise young children constantly.

Only half of all aquatic fatalities occur during the summer (Smith and Smith 1994); the rest occur throughout the remainder of the year. Many victims are nonswimmers who are fishers, hunters, canoeists, and kayakers who frequently underestimate the weather conditions. They also tend to underestimate air and water temperatures and their personal limitations. The remoteness of the activities involved complicates rescues and emergency medical care. And if the problems are not great enough, many of these victims further compound their situations because they do not know how to swim or are poor swimmers, consume alcoholic beverages, and do not wear personal flotation devices. Particularly in the remote settings where people hunt, fish, and explore, preventing aquatic accidents is much easier and more crucial than responding to them.

IN APRIL 2001, TWO MEN IN AN INFLATABLE BOAT IN PUGET SOUND were ejected from the vessel when the driver made a sharp turn. They were only 200 yards from shore, but one of them perished and the other had to be hospitalized after being rescued by a water rescue team. Empty alcoholic beverage containers were found in the boat. Neither victim wore a personal flotation device. The law of drowning held firm—when you ignore the rules, you pay the ultimate price.

Response

Remember the basic rules of rescue set forth in chapter 2. First, assessment of the situation is critical. Do your best to determine what happened. Question bystanders while you prepare to rescue the victim. Analyze the situation. Is a spinal injury a consideration? Is more than one person in distress? Has anyone summoned aid? Is rescue or first aid equipment available? What resources are available? What is the status of the victim? Gather as much information as you can in about 10 seconds and then form a brief plan of action. If other people are present, delegate some responsibilities.

Use the least hazardous method to rescue a swimmer. When the person needing to be rescued is conscious, rational, and near shore, extending an object or throwing a line or float may be effective. When the victim is unconscious, panicked, or distant, you must go to the victim. Use a watercraft whenever possible. Remember that physically entering the water to rescue someone is the least desirable method. Swimming rescues can result in two fatalities—yours and the victim's.

If you feel that there is no choice other than a swimming rescue, you should attempt such a rescue only if you are trained in swimming rescue techniques, have practiced the techniques within the past year, and have flotation to support you and the victim. When one swimmer attempts to rescue another swimmer in distress without flotation, the result is often tragic. There is a difference between taking a calculated risk and taking a foolish risk. Yours should be calculated.

Tether Lines

If you cannot throw a rescue line to a victim, consider taking the line with you when you swim to the victim's aid. Professional rescuers use a tether line attached to a harness. A tether line reduces the effort needed to return to safety and can be invaluable in moving water (see figure 6.4).

You are not likely to have a tether harness for a swimming rescue situation. Avoid tying the line to yourself because a tether line must have quick-release capability or it could become a liability in some circumstances. Do use a tether line if you can, but tie it to your rescue float instead of to you.

Figure 6.4 When there are currents or wind, a tether line clipped to a harness is invaluable for helping a rescuer return to a rescue vessel, especially when assisting a victim.

I recommend that rescue swimmers use flexible torpedo rescue buoys that can be clipped around a victim. The tether line is clipped to the line attached to the rescue float (see figure 6.5). The rescue swimmer maintains contact with the victim while both are pulled to safety using the tether line. With this configuration, the rescue swimmer can disconnect the victim, if necessary, and the rescuer is free to move without being encumbered by the tether line, which can become a hindrance during rescue exits onto a vessel.

Figure 6.5 A tether line clipped to a rescue float helps get the rescuer and victim back to safety, especially when the water is moving.

A tether line is most effective when an assistant is available to manage the end of the line on shore or aboard a boat. The assistant keeps slack from the line and, when signaled, pulls the line to retrieve the rescuer and victim. Retrieving a swimmer with or without a victim using a tether line is a skill that must be developed and practiced. The assistant must pull slowly and steadily. Jerking the line can pull the float from the grasp of the rescuer. The density of water creates so much resistance that rapid movement can weaken the rescuer's grasp on the float and cause separation. Losing contact with the rescue float can be very serious, especially in moving water.

Swimmer Assists

Unless the victim is incapacitated, a rescuer may be able help a victim reach safety with minimal assistance. Consider assists instead of rescues whenever possible. Assists help victims maintain some confidence, while rescues do not. The steps of assisting are simple. Establishing buoyancy is the first and most critical step, which is why a rescue float is essential. The second step—reducing activity and gaining control of breathing—is not possible if the victim is not supported. When the victim recovers from breathing distress, discussion of a solution to the situation is possible. The rescuer and the victim agree on a plan of action and implement it. Often an effective rescuer can talk a person in distress to safety using words of encouragement. I advocate getting those in distress to do as much as possible individually by providing verbal, but not physical, assistance. Take physical action only when victims are not capable of independent action.

Even physical assists do not need to be full-blown rescues where you merely tow a victim to safety. A tired swimmer's carry or a biceps push—both described in chapter 2—can make a rescue better than a tow for both parties. Remember the criteria for an effective transport. You should be able to swim easily, maintain eye contact with the victim, and communicate with the victim. Assists and rescues should not be silent. Rescuers should talk to victims periodically, reporting progress and providing reassurance. Watching the victim's eyes provides information about the person's emotional state. Many rescuers force excited victims into a horizontal position in the water. The added stress of the uncomfortable position can cause the stressed victim to panic because distressed people want to be in an upright position. An exhausted swimmer who has flotation and has regained breathing control may be capable of assuming a horizontal position for a tired swimmer's carry, but a weak swimmer who believes that she is about to drown will panic and struggle in desperation if the rescuer attempts horizontal positioning. Discussing what you will do and agreeing before you take action is important. Assessing the person's reaction to the actions taken is just as important. If your plan isn't working, stop, discuss the matter, and agree on a different course of action. Assists and rescues often are dynamic and changing. Strive to be flexible.

Swimming Rescues

A water-based rescue of an incapacitated swimmer in deep, rough water can be extremely challenging. Rescuers must have floatation and should have swim fins, which help immensely. The rescuer should also have a rescue breathing mask. Just a few inexpensive items of rescue equipment readily available can make a tremendous difference.

Supporting an incapacitated swimmer requires training and practice. If the victim is vertical in the water and struggling, extend the float and push it beneath the victim's hands. The person will instinctively grab the float and climb on it. You will need to position the float beneath an incapacitated individual. Techniques vary with the type of float and the rescue situation. When you use a surf mat or air mattress as a flotation device, you can swim on top of a victim who is face down in the water, hug the victim, and roll over. The victim will end up on top of the air mattress and you will be beneath it. Slide from beneath the mattress and you will surface beside the victim. Use this method only when you are certain the victim has not suffered a spinal injury.

When you use a flexible torpedo tube float, which is my personal favorite, grasp one end of the float, push it down and under the victim, and release the end. Attempt to push the distant end of the float farther than the width of the victim's body to center the float beneath the victim. When you release the end, it should float up and appear on the other side of the victim. Push or pull on

Figure 6.6 Support a victim in calm water by balancing him on a rescue float. If the water is rough, clip the float around the victim.

the end nearest you to balance the victim on the float. You should be able to balance the victim on a single float as shown in figure 6.6.

Assess an unconscious victim for breathing. If the victim is not breathing and you can get the person out of the water rapidly, do so. If you cannot extricate the victim rapidly, clear any water from the victim's airway and begin rescue breathing in the water. The task of aquatic rescue breathing is far easier with a rescue breathing mask than with mouth-to-mouth or mouth-to-nose techniques (see figure 6.7). The procedure also keeps the victim's airway drier. Rescue breathing is difficult, but not impossible, when you are not wearing swim fins. When you practice aquatic rescue breathing, you will rapidly learn the significant value of swim fins and a rescue breathing mask. Do not bother to check for a pulse because you will not be able to detect one and you cannot administer CPR effectively in the water.

You must also consider other factors discussed in this book, such as spinal injury management, heat loss, and the best means of extrication. You must be able to think clearly while performing complex physical activities. The only way to do so is to practice the physical skills until you can do them almost without

Figure 6.7 If you must perform rescue breathing in the water, the use of a rescue breathing mask is the best technique.

thinking. When your skills are automatic, you will be able to use your mind for analysis. This fundamental principle is why professionals are able to function calmly in stressful situations. Their skills are polished so their demeanor is calm and they are able to think clearly.

First Aid

When a swimmer suffers a submersion injury, you must keep several problems in mind. A clear airway, adequate breathing, and circulation are the first priorities (remember ABC), but you must also treat the victim for hypothermia. A victim can rapidly become hypothermic in water that seems warm. Bear in mind that in the process of drowning or nearly drowning the victim swallows a significant amount of water. Cold water in the stomach and possibly in the lungs can lower core temperature quickly. The temperature of the water at the surface and the temperature of the water at the bottom where a victim is recovered may differ substantially. Always treat swimming victims for heat loss. Get them dry, bundle them up, and deliver heated oxygen when possible. See chapter 9 for information about providing heated oxygen in the field.

Another concern is the swimmer who has lost consciousness in the water or has apparently aspirated water. A victim who has become unconscious while in water or is coughing after breathing water requires medical attention. Life-threatening complications can develop if the victim does not receive a medical evaluation. A victim may be embarrassed and decline a trip to the hospital, but you must be persuasive. Do your absolute best to convince submersion injury victims that they need medical attention even if they feel that all is well following an incident.

Key Points

To prevent and successfully handle swimming injuries, swimmers and rescuers alike should do the following:

- Know the environment—currents, waves, temperatures, depths, and hazards. Get an orientation to new or unfamiliar areas.
- Avoid rough water and poor weather conditions.
- Consider a helmet for head protection.
- Be well nourished when engaging in aquatic activities.
- Beware of heat loss!
- Know your personal limits and remain within them.
- Hyperventilate no more than three breaths before breath-hold swims.
- Avoid diving headfirst into unknown or shallow water.
- Avoid the consumption of alcohol when in or around water.
- Move with water, not against it.
- Swim at designated beaches staffed by lifeguards.
- Assume a feet-first position when adrift in rough water.
- Avoid clinging to stationary objects in cold, swift water.
- Do not swim in canals.
- Avoid drains in swimming pools.
- Do your best to prevent cramps, recognize early warning signs of cramps, and relieve cramps promptly.
- Resist challenges to swim to distant target objects or to race in open water.
- Avoid toy buoyancy devices. Do wear approved personal flotation devices.
- Restrict children's access to water and supervise them constantly.
- Be prepared (trained, practiced, and equipped) to rescue a swimmer in distress.
- Assist distressed swimmers whenever possible. Rescue only those who are unable to overcome their difficulty without assistance.

Chapter 7

Scuba Diving Injuries

Drowning is the number one cause of death for divers, although drowning often is a terminal event precipitated by other causes. According to the Divers Alert Network, the most frequent causes of diving accidents are insufficient air, entrapment, cardiovascular problems, intoxication, and cerebral arterial gas embolism (CAGE or simply air embolism) (Divers Alert Network 2001). My accident investigation experience suggests that many medical examiners are not familiar with the special protocol required for the autopsy of the victim of a scuba diving accident. Since divers die in water and there is evidence of drowning, autopsy reports typically state the cause of death as drowning when other contributing factors could be discovered with correct autopsy procedures. When you become familiar with the causes of scuba diving accidents and the differences between swimmers and divers in rescue situations, you will understand why the rescue techniques for divers are unique. With that understanding you can learn proven rescue techniques for scuba diving. All aquatic personnel who may have occasion to rescue scuba divers should complete scuba diving training and obtain scuba certification. Appendix A contains a list of diver training organizations that sanction scuba training. All rescuers will find many techniques described in this chapter to be helpful for rescuing swimmers as well.

Diving rescues involve prevention, recognition, assists, rescues, first aid, accident management, and evacuation. This chapter deals with situations in which you need to take immediate action to assist or rescue a diver who is on the verge of drowning. Chapters 9, 10, and 11 address first aid, evacuation, and accident management. You can learn prevention techniques by completing a diving rescue techniques course of instruction.

Learning Goals *By the end of this chapter, you should be able to:*

- ▶ Describe several differences between rescues required for scuba divers and rescues typically required for swimmers.
- ▶ State two scuba diving–related illnesses that require treatment in a recompression chamber.
- ▶ List six of seven traditional scuba diving rescue misconceptions.
- ▶ List six of eight signs that indicate that a diver at the surface is in extreme distress.
- ▶ List seven of eight signs that indicate a diver underwater is in extreme distress.
- ▶ List six of eight indications that a scuba diving rescue is necessary.
- ▶ List various questions to ask yourself and bystanders if a dive rescue situation occurs.
- ▶ List six actions that can be taken in advance to prepare for scuba diving rescues.
- ▶ Define oxygen debt and explain how to minimize its effects.
- ▶ List six of eight things to look for when you approach a distressed scuba diver in the water.
- ▶ List two effective means of establishing communication with a scuba diver who is in distress.
- ▶ Describe how to get a distressed scuba diver to discard an item worn or held.
- ▶ Describe two types of noncontact assists.
- ▶ Demonstrate the contact support position.
- ▶ List the order of preference for establishing buoyancy for a distressed scuba diver.
- ▶ List three ways to prevent a distressed scuba diver from grabbing you and explain how to free yourself if you are grabbed.
- ▶ List six of eight problems typically experienced by distressed scuba divers.
- ▶ Describe two types of swimming assists for scuba diving rescues.
- ▶ Explain how to rescue a submerged, unconscious scuba diver.
- ▶ List three methods of aquatic rescue breathing for scuba diving rescues.
- ▶ List four of five disadvantages of the "do-si-do" method of rescue breathing.
- ▶ Describe the ABCDE method of aquatic rescue breathing.
- ▶ Explain the basic sequence of equipment removal for a scuba diving rescue.
- ▶ Describe three self-rescue techniques for scuba divers.

Diving Differences

Scuba diving often takes place at remote, rugged locations where there are no lifeguards and where it may be difficult to access for the emergency medical service (EMS). The water may be rougher and deeper than that frequented by swimmers. A distressed diver may be entangled or entrapped. The diver's air supply may be contaminated with carbon monoxide. Divers usually pursue their activity in pairs. If you rescue one diver, you need to account for and perhaps rescue the victim's partner.

Scuba divers are not likely to have neck injuries. Sixteen years of diving accident reports for the two largest diver training organizations, annual diving accident reports published by the Divers Alert Network (DAN), and a widespread survey of the scuba diving community failed to disclose a single instance of a diving accident involving a neck injury (Survey in the PADI Undersea Journal by Dennis Graver). The finding is significant because some in-water rescue breathing techniques for scuba divers support the victim's head with a neck lift. On the other hand, if you find an unconscious diver floating in the surf zone, you might suspect a neck injury and should do all you can to stabilize the person's neck before removing him from the water.

The equipment that allows divers to adapt to the underwater environment can be a hindrance in an emergency. Although divers wear exposure suits, they lose body heat slowly over time. Slow cooling of the body impairs rather than aids an injured diver when an accident occurs. Divers in distress may have air to breathe from scuba equipment, but frequently reject the equipment when panicked. Divers have several means to establish buoyancy, but may fail to get buoyant when in distress. Weight that enables divers to descend can suddenly prevent them from moving upward in the water. To a diver in control, equipment feels comfortable; to a diver in distress, the same equipment may feel confining and restricting and contribute to stress and panic (see figure 7.1).

Divers often fail to take self-help action when distress begins. They certainly fail to help themselves when instinctive drowning behavior begins. Failure to take prompt action to establish buoyancy before instinctive survival behavior takes control explains why many diving victims lack buoyancy when rescued or recovered. When distressed divers use their hands for survival movements, they cannot use them for any other purpose.

Divers breathe compressed air, which expands as surrounding pressure decreases during an ascent. A conscious, breath-holding, panicked diver is likely to experience a burst lung while attempting to reach the surface. A lung overexpansion injury can cause a diver to lose consciousness during ascent or shortly after surfacing. A burst lung can create a life-threatening emergency. Prompt recompression in a hyperbaric chamber is the only treatment for air embolism—the worst of the lung overexpansion injuries (see figure 7.2). Signs and symptoms of air embolism are similar to those of a stroke (see chapter 4).

Depending on time, depth, and ascent-rate parameters, an ascending diver may develop decompression sickness, a malady that occurs when gas dissolved

Figure 7.1 Diving equipment that normally aids a person in the water can be a hindrance in an emergency.

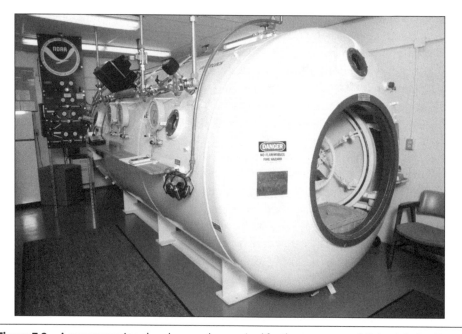

Figure 7.2 A recompression chamber may be required for the treatment of diving injuries. Know the location of the nearest chamber.

in the body under pressure comes out of solution too rapidly. Victims of decompression sickness—commonly called "bends"—also require treatment in a recompression chamber. Symptoms of bends range from joint pain to numbness and weakness to paralysis and unconsciousness (Graver 1999).

Divers also experience the cardiopulmonary emergencies presented in chapter 4. Exertion, slow cooling, and physical and mental stress are combining factors that may precipitate heart rhythm abnormalities or a heart attack.

SCUBA DIVERS CAN BLACK OUT if their breathing gas does not contain a sufficient amount of oxygen. A man in Florida used a scuba tank that had been in his garage for years to dive in a canal behind his home. He drowned because water inside the tank had caused corrosion, which had depleted the oxygen in the compressed air. The man breathed only nitrogen, and because he was exhaling carbon dioxide, he had no indication that his breathing was inadequate. Problems with mixed gas rebreathers can also lead to blackouts. Self-contained breathing apparatus must be well maintained.

Traditional Rescue Techniques

Diving rescues have occurred since people started diving. Some of the early rescue methods and first aid procedures, which were based on incorrect assumptions, persist today. The purpose of this section is to identify outdated scuba diving rescue techniques and theories and discourage their use.

A diver in distress may grab and hold a rescuer, but it is a misconception that a panicked diver will attempt to grasp someone. As Frank Pia indicates, you can get face to face with a panicked person in the water (Pia 1974). The only movements made by a person exhibiting instinctive drowning behavior are thrusting the arms out to the sides and down and kicking weakly. Some individuals believe it is better to allow a panicked diver to lose consciousness than to make physical contact with the person. If a diver is struggling weakly and on the verge of drowning, make physical contact and keep them above water. If you allow the person to aspirate water, you decrease your chances of saving the person.

Another commonly held myth is that you must vent the air from the lungs of an unconscious diver during ascent. Would-be rescuers frequently tilt back the head of a nonbreathing diver to ensure an open airway. Some rescuers advocate squeezing the injured diver to help expel the air. Proponents of such actions believe expansion of the air in the lungs during a rescue ascent can cause lung overexpansion with its attendant serious injuries. Dr. George Harpur (1974) described why an unconscious scuba diver will not suffer a lung overexpansion injury. He proved that it is only difficult to get air into an unconscious person; air will come out of an unconscious person easily regardless of head position. Attempts to maintain an open airway for an unconscious scuba diver may permit water to enter the victim's lungs.

The most common methods of in-water rescue breathing have inadequate jaw support to maintain an open airway for a victim. A lack of jaw support allows air from rescue breaths to go into the stomach as well as the lungs. The Royal Surf Lifesaving Association and St. Johns Ambulance organizations of Australia agree that the common "do-si-do" in-water rescue breathing technique—described later in this chapter—does not appear to adequately support or lift the jaw. Whenever possible, rescue breathing in the water should use a technique that lifts the chin—an action that helps to reduce gastric distention (Letter from Hans Telford, Training Department, NAUI Australia, December 1991).

The standard rate for artificial respiration on land is 12 breaths per minute—one breath every five seconds. This is too rapid for the logistics of water rescue situations. A more appropriate rate for in-water rescues is two breaths every 10 seconds. Since one person giving CPR to a patient ventilates at a rate of two breaths every 15 compressions, a rescuer in the water can administer two breaths every 10 seconds, which is the same time interval as CPR. The British Sub-Aqua Club suggests a rate of two breaths every 15 seconds (British Sub-Aqua Club 1987, 40). Physicians, rescue experts, and Red Cross Headquarters staff members attending a near drowning workshop in October 1990 in San Diego, California, agreed unanimously with the two-per-ten rate. The advantages of the two-per-ten rate are as follows:

- The rescuer does not tire as quickly.
- The exhalation volume of the rescuer will be larger for a longer period of time.
- The rescuer can remove equipment more expediently.
- The rescuer can tow the victim to an exit point more quickly.
- The number of opportunities for water to enter the victim during ventilations is one-half that of the one-per-five rate.

During a 1993 diving rescue workshop in Seattle, Washington, 100 participants were asked, without bias, to try in-water ventilation rates of one breath every five seconds and two breaths every 10 seconds and state which rate they preferred. Eighty-seven of the 100 rescuers preferred the two-per-ten rate for the reasons previously stated.

Another common first aid practice is to check the pulse of an unconscious person. Many rescuers mistakenly believe that the procedure applies to in-water rescues. When you rescue a diver, you should delay pulse checking until you remove the injured person from the water (American Heart Association 2000, 236). Divers frequently wear hoods and gloves. Cold water dulls normal tactile sense. The pulse of a near-drowned person may be as slow as several beats per minute! Because in-water rescues are strenuous, if you do feel a pulse, it is likely to be yours. After you remove a person from the water, you need to get someone warm and dry who knows the procedure to feel for a pulse. Do not waste precious time and energy trying to find a pulse while in the water.

Dr. Henry Heimlich (1981) recommends subdiaphragmatic pressure (the Heimlich maneuver) to expel water from the lungs of drowning persons. Several authoritative articles state that the Heimlich maneuver has no place in the initial therapy of a nearly drowned person unless a rescuer is unable to ventilate the victim (American Heart Association 2000, 234; Orlowski 1987; Ornato 1986). The attendees of the 1990 near drowning workshop in San Diego, California, agreed with the position stated in the articles.

In-water cardiopulmonary resuscitation (CPR) is ineffective (American Heart Association 2000, 236). If you believe that an injured person needs CPR, you must first remove her from the water and place her on a firm surface. Since you cannot detect a pulse in the water, your best course of action is to remove the person from the water as quickly as possible. When you cannot remove a person from the water within two to three minutes after respiratory arrest, administer rescue breathing in the water continuously in case the person does have circulation. The two-per-ten ventilation rate speeds the process of getting the injured person onto a firm surface better than an interval of one breath every five seconds.

Modern Rescue Techniques

A better understanding of physiology, new studies, new equipment, and more effective rescue techniques provide better means for saving lives. This section describes the most current diving rescue techniques.

Recognition

Divers usually drown quietly. A diver signaling for assistance needs aid, but probably does not need to be rescued. A panicked diver on the verge of drowning does not call for help, wave an arm, inflate a signal tube, blow a whistle, or fire a flare. A panicked diver will not establish buoyancy, breathe properly, or follow instructions (see figures 7.3, 7.4, and 7.5). You must recognize the signs of extreme distress (Professional Association of Diving Instructors 1985) and respond quickly to prevent a drowning (see table 7.1).

Signs of distress often precede those of extreme distress. The following behaviors indicate a diver who may soon exhibit signs of distress. Be alert and be prepared to render aid if you see a diver do any of the following:

- Surface down current from the exit area
- Surface a long distance from the exit area
- Lag far behind another diver during a surface swim
- Struggle with a heavy load
- Cough, choke, or vomit uncontrollably
- Exert to remain high in the water
- Cling and climb in an attempt to get out of the water
- Sink immediately after surfacing

Figure 7.3 Distressed divers use an inflatable tube and other means to signal for assistance at the surface, but panicked divers do not signal for help.

Figure 7.4 A diver in distress at the surface.

Figure 7.5 An overweighted diver breathing heavily and on the verge of distress. Note diagonal position relative to horizontal diver in background.

Table 7.1 Signs of a Diver in Extreme Distress

At the surface	Underwater
Low, vertical position in the water (lack of buoyancy)	Bolting to the surface
Mask and mouthpiece removed	Rejection of mask and mouthpiece
Head back and chin up	Arm swimming replacing leg propulsion
Gasping for air	Continuous bubbles from exhaust (rapid breathing)
Eyes closed tightly or opened very wide	Wide, wild eyes
Quick, jerky movements	Quick, jerky movements or convulsions
No response to signals or questions	Failure to respond to signals
Alone and motionless	Alone and motionless with no exhaust bubbles

Initial Response

When you believe drowning is imminent, go to the distressed person. Divers in distress may grasp lines or floats thrown to them, but a panicked diver about to drown will not grasp anything unless you place the object beneath his submerged arms. Assess the situation and decide whether the diver needs assistance or needs to be rescued (see figure 7.6). If you believe the person is about to drown, do not waste time with assisting techniques. Go rescue the victim.

Determine whether you can assist the distressed diver without unduly endangering yourself. Are you qualified for the circumstances, and do you feel capable of managing the situation? Bear in mind that would-be rescuers can become victims. You should feel confident that you can help the distressed person without placing yourself in peril.

If you decide to act, quickly assess the environmental conditions. How rough is the water? What is the approximate temperature of the water? Is the water clear or turbid? What is the approximate depth at the distressed diver's location? How far away is the person? Are there hazards such as rocks or surf? By taking a few moments for assessment, you can avoid the empty feeling of being ill equipped when you reach the person in distress.

Rescue equipment is always helpful, but sometimes equipment is essential. You need exposure protection for cold water. Use fins whenever possible. Wear a mask and snorkel. Use scuba equipment for a deep-water rescue.

You must act quickly in an emergency. There may not be time to don all of the equipment you should have for a rescue. Consider wearing your exposure suit while you stand near the water. Have remaining dive equipment set up and positioned for immediate use. If you practice donning your equipment quickly and have it ready for use, you can prepare for a rescue in a matter of seconds while giving instructions to people in the area.

What rescue equipment is at hand? Is there a boat pole that you can extend to a panicked diver? Is a line or any flotation device available that you can tow with you when you go to the rescue? Is there anything that you can use to make rescue breathing in the water easier and more effective? How will you get an unconscious diver out of the water? Is any first aid equipment available for use after the rescue? Try to answer these questions before an emergency occurs. Prepare for rescues. If you only have to rescue someone once, your preparation efforts will have been worthwhile.

The following factors influence your initial rescue response:

- Your personal safety
- Environmental conditions
- Diving equipment readily available
- Rescue equipment readily available
- Other people in the vicinity

Figure 7.6   Initial rescue response.

Who are the people at the site? Do any of them have special training or qualifications for an emergency? Are the people willing to get involved? Do they know the location of the phone or radio, how to operate the device, who to call, the phone numbers or radio frequencies, and how to request emergency aid? Talking to people before an accident and establishing a plan of action for an emergency is better than trying to coordinate a plan hastily during a crisis.

The more you can prepare in advance to respond to a diving emergency, the easier rescuing someone will be. Sometimes you may be prepared, and sometimes you may have to respond to an emergency without preparation. The procedures described in this chapter range from a swimmer rescuing a scuba diver to a trained rescue diver rescuing another scuba diver. You will learn techniques for assisted and unassisted rescues. There is no set way to rescue a diver that works for every situation. You will learn a variety of techniques. Hopefully you will never have to use any of the procedures, but if you do, you will be prepared for a successful rescue.

All you may need to do for some divers in trouble is to reach them (see figure 7.7). Fully equipped divers without fins have little means of propulsion

Figure 7.7 If you act quickly, you may be able to rescue a diver just by reaching him.

because diving footwear streamlines their feet and reduces kicking efficiency. A nonbuoyant diver without fins who lets go of a boat during an exit in a current may panic quickly. You can avert disaster by extending a pole to the diver or by jumping into the water, holding the stern of the boat, and extending your legs to the distressed person. You must assess the situation rapidly and act quickly because the time you have may be only a few seconds.

You may need to swim to the rescue. After you recognize an emergency and before you enter the water, equip yourself as well as the situation permits and delegate responsibilities to others. In some situations you should don fins before entering the water; in other circumstances you should wade well into the water before donning your fins. Sometimes you should run along the shore before entering the water so you can reduce the distance to the person in distress. You can move faster on land than you can in the water. Assess the situation and determine the best course of action. As you enter the water and swim to the distressed diver, keep your eyes on the person continuously. Try to find a distant object behind the person so you will have an imaginary line to follow if the person submerges before you can reach him. If possible, assign spotters to point to the exact location of the victim (see figure 7.8). If the person submerges, the spotters can direct you to the point at which the person was last seen.

You need to reach a distressed diver quickly, but be sure to pace yourself during your initial swim. If you exert excessively while swimming to the rescue, you

Figure 7.8 If you can, assign spotters to fix the location of a victim in case the person sinks before you can reach him.

will become breathless and unable to assist the person in distress. Your muscles can require large quantities of oxygen before your circulation and respiration adjust to meet the increased demands of an activity. The result is an "oxygen debt" and the need to stop and catch your breath. Keep in mind that after you reach the person's location, you may have to hold your breath and dive beneath the surface to recover the person. Minimize the oxygen debt by pacing your activity.

Approaches

Evaluate the condition and plight of a distressed diver during your approach swim. Watch the distressed diver continually. Here are some actions and items to look for:

1. How far is the person's head above water? Is the individual high in the water and treading strongly or low in the water and moving weakly?

2. Has the person submerged momentarily or aspirated water?

3. Does the individual appear to be alert, panicked, or incapacitated?

4. Is the distressed diver holding anything in her hands? Items typically carried by divers are cameras, spear guns, game bags, dive lights, and salvaged objects.

5. What are the person's hand, arm, foot, and leg movements? Are they quick and jerky or controlled and deliberate?

6. What is the distressed diver's respiratory condition? Is she gasping or breathing rapidly?

7. Is the diver's mask missing or on her forehead?

8. What type of equipment is the diver wearing? How is it configured? What type of releases does the equipment have? Where are the releases located?

Determine as much as you can above the surface while you approach the distressed diver from a distance. As you get closer to the person, look beneath the surface to assess the situation further. Stop beyond the distressed person's reach to complete your assessment, attempt communication, and determine a plan of action.

Try to establish communication with the person to get her to take corrective action. Communication is the key. If you cannot communicate with the person (ask a question and get a response), rescue her at once. Yelling at a distressed diver is ineffective. It can increase stress if the person has not panicked, and it has no effect if the person is already panicked. An effective method to communicate with a distressed diver is to ask questions (see figure 7.9).

Often, distressed divers will not discard objects that contribute to their problem (e.g., their weights), but they will give the objects to you if you ask for them. Ask the victim to give you her weights, camera, spear gun, or "treasure." You can then discard the items and help the diver! The person that you assist may be angry with you later because you ditched something of value, but accepting the anger of a proud diver is better than risking the person's life.

1. Are you OK?

2. Would you like some help?

3. What's your name?

4. Are you having any difficulty?

5. Can you make yourself bouyant?

6. Where is your buddy?

7. Can you hear me?

8. Would you put some air in your buoyancy compensator (BC)?

9. Would you hand me your weight belt?

Figure 7.9   Examples of appropriate questions to ask a distressed diver.

If you receive no reply to your questions—not even a nod of the head—try to gain the person's attention by threatening to leave. If you say, "I'm here to help, but if you don't listen to me, I'm leaving," and then turn as if to leave, the individual in distress may blurt, "Wait!" When you get someone in distress to speak, you have communicated and may be able to assist the person. When distressed people speak to you, you can instruct them about what to do to cope with their difficulties.

Determine a plan of action as you complete your assessment. You have more time to assess when a distressed diver is high in the water, breathing hard, and moving strongly than when the person is low in the water, gasping, and moving weakly. If the victim appears to be moving strongly, stop during your approach; but if the victim's movements are weak, you must make contact with the distressed person as soon as possible. If you believe drowning is imminent, go to the person immediately.

Noncontact Assists

Assists may be noncontact or contact. Obviously, you should try noncontact assists first because they present less risk for you. When you approach a distressed diver and he moves toward you, ask questions as you back away. You may be able to keep the person moving toward you all the way to safety. It feels good when a person whom you talked to safety asks, "Why didn't you help me?" and you explain that you helped him to help himself. You also allow people to save face and gain some confidence when you help them manage their problems.

An extension is a noncontact assist. When you swim to the distressed diver, take a line or a float with you and extend the line or float to the person. When you are wearing a flotation device and believe that the person in distress will be able to remain at the surface, remove your flotation and extend it to the victim. Place extended objects beneath the outstretched arms of a distressed diver. Allow the person to grasp the object and then back away while you give the person reassurance and instructions.

Don't waste time with extensions if you feel the distressed person is about to drown. You need to make contact with the individual. The following section explains how to rescue a struggling person while minimizing personal risk.

Contact Assists

A person about to drown needs support. When you do not have a float, but can reach the person at the surface, make yourself buoyant, if possible. If you have a weight belt, discard it. If you have a buoyancy control device (BCD), inflate it. When you make contact with a diver in distress, use your left hand to grasp the top of the left wrist or forearm of the individual and pull her toward you. Place your right hand under the person's left armpit and lift her while you position yourself beside her. This is the "contact support" position (see figure 7.10). From the support position you can inflate the person's BCD; release the weight belt; and support, reassure, and communicate.

a

b

c

Figure 7.10 The three steps of the contact support position: *(a)* Grasp the person's left wrist with your left hand, *(b)* pull the person toward you and provide support with your right hand under the person's left arm, and *(c)* position yourself at the person's left side and establish buoyancy.

Your first diving rescue goal is to make the distressed diver buoyant. You have several options for establishing buoyancy. The options, in order of preference, are as follows:

1. *Discard the distressed diver's weights.* Most divers wear weights on belts around their waists. Some divers have weights integrated into their scuba units. A belt should have a quick release that opens to the right (see figure 7.11*a*). When you examine the equipment, you should be able to idenfity a quick release for integrated weights. When you release a weight belt, be sure that you pull it well clear of the wearer before discarding. There are many places on a scuba diver where a dropped belt can snag. Murphy's law applies—If there is any way for the weights to hang up, they will.

2. *Partially inflate the distressed diver's BCD using the low-pressure inflator.* Most scuba divers today use BCDs that have a low-pressure hose between the scuba tank and the BCD hose, which is on the left side of the device. The BCD control valve has two buttons: one for inflation and one for deflation (see figure 7.11*b*).

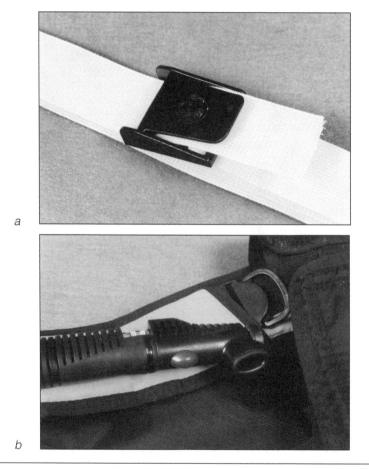

a

b

Figure 7.11 It helps to be familiar with diving equipment, especially *(a)* weight releases *(b)* and BCD control valves.

When you push the inflation button, you can hear air enter the BCD. If you push the wrong button, simply try the other one. Avoid complete inflation of the BCD because some devices squeeze the distressed diver when fully inflated and increase stress and panic.

3. *Partially inflate the distressed diver's BCD orally.* If the diver does not have a low-pressure inflator or if the inflator does not function, you can inflate the BCD orally from beside or behind the person. Place the mouthpiece in your mouth, depress one of the buttons on the valve, and exhale. If the air does not enter the BCD, depress the other button. Exhale several breaths into the BCD.

4. *Activate the diver's BCD gas cartridge detonator.* The BCD may have a carbon dioxide cartridge and detonator for rapid inflation, but the detonators are unreliable, especially with saltwater exposure. The sudden, complete inflation of the BCD may feel confining and cause a distressed diver to panic. Pull the cord to activate the cartridge only as a last resort.

Defenses and Releases

It is better to prevent a distressed diver from grabbing you than it is to free yourself from the clutches of someone who believes that he is about to drown. It helps to approach a struggling person from behind because you can control a person better from the rear than from the front, but you may not be able to circle behind the person at the surface. You may approach a diver underwater during the last few feet of a rescue swim. Consider approaching a distressed diver from the front initially because you can reach up and in and release the diver's weights or push a button to inflate the BCD (see figure 7.12).

Figure 7.12 An initial front approach underwater may be an effective way to establish buoyancy quickly.

The contact support position is a good defensive arrangement. You can feel the distressed person's anxiety and movements with your right hand around the person's left arm (see figure 7.13). If you feel the distressed individual turn toward you, quickly raise your left arm and place your left elbow between your head and the person's head to block her attempts to grab you. When you turn and place your elbow beside the person's head, your left hand will be behind her head. Reach behind the diver with your left hand, grasp her scuba tank valve or BCD collar, move behind her, and help her establish buoyancy; then get her to calm down.

You may not be able to prevent a distressed person from grabbing you. Keep in mind that the person has one objective—to get above water. A distressed diver will climb anything, including you, for elevation. A good technique to get a struggling individual to release you is to move downward, which is the opposite direction the person wants to go. Push the person up to push yourself down.

A rescuer with scuba equipment can breathe while underwater, but a struggling diver may knock the regulator from the rescuer's mouth. A scuba regulator dangling beside a struggling diver may be useful to you as a rescuer. Scuba divers in distress frequently have functioning scuba equipment, but reject it. You may be able to breathe from the distressed diver's scuba unit while providing assistance.

Problem Solving

After you establish buoyancy for the distressed diver, your next objective is to get the person to regain respiratory control. Rapid, shallow, ineffective breathing (hy-

Figure 7.13　The defensive position for the contact support position.

poventilation) is one of the major problems contributing to stress and causing panic. Reassure the distressed diver and get him to stop struggling and to breathe deeply. Allow the person to breathe without a snorkel or regulator, which impedes airflow somewhat. When the individual overcomes respiratory distress, he will calm down, you will be able to communicate, and you can address any problems that remain. The following list identifies typical distressed scuba diver problems:

- Lack of buoyancy
- Breathing difficulty owing to a tight wet suit, aspiration of water, poorly maintained equipment, or a medical problem
- Equipment difficulties, such as a slipping weight belt, the scuba tank slipping from the backpack, a BCD that rides up, or the inability to retrieve a regulator
- Equipment malfunction, such as a broken strap, a stuck BCD or dry suit inflator valve, or a free-flowing regulator
- Equipment loss
- Entanglement
- Sudden, acute, disabling illness or injury
- Panic

Your problem-solving objective is, whenever possible, to help a distressed diver overcome the difficulty and proceed unassisted. Help the person identify the problem, determine possible ways to resolve the problem, select an appropriate response to the difficulty, and manage the situation. Assist people, but allow them to do as much for themselves as possible. Allow them to preserve some dignity and learn from the experience.

You may relieve a cramp, which usually occurs in a diver's leg, by stretching and applying steady pressure to the contracted muscle. Grasp the person's fin with one hand and gently push it toward the person's shin to stretch the calf muscle. Grasp the person's calf muscle with your other hand to obtain leverage and press on the muscle. Avoid kneading or massaging.

Swimming Assists

You may have to transport a conscious, breathing, physically incapacitated person. The person may be exhausted or injured and unable to reach the exit point unassisted. An effective swimming assist should meet the following criteria:

- The distressed diver is comfortable, secure, and able to breathe easily.
- The rescuer has physical control of and eye-to-eye contact with the distressed diver, can talk to the person, and can kick effectively.

Pulling assists are not acceptable. Pushes are effective because they meet the assist criteria. Figure 7.14 depicts two good assisting techniques—the fin push and the biceps push.

a

b

Figure 7.14 The *(a)* fin push and the *(b)* biceps push assists meet essential criteria for swimming assists.

When a person is exhausted or injured, but calm, use the fin push to assist her to the exit point. Have the diver lie on her back and breathe through the mouth, place the diver's fins on your shoulders, and push her. When a person is injured seriously, has nearly drowned, or is anxious and agitated, use the biceps push. An excited diver will not want to lie back, so don't waste time with positioning attempts. Grasp the distressed diver's armpit with your closest hand (thumb pointing up), get close to the person, and start pushing and talking while you swim.

Pace yourself while you swim. Slow, steady movement is better than quick spurts. Rest occasionally as needed. Get assistance if you can because it is more than twice as easy for two people to transport a diver. Try to use a rescue line. Being slowly pulled to the exit is much easier than swimming.

Surfacing an Unconscious Diver

You may not be able to reach a distressed diver before he loses consciousness and sinks. Do your best to prevent sinking because the survival rate for divers who sink is extremely low. If a diver sinks, you must get the person to the surface as soon as possible. When you have to bring an unconscious diver to the surface, use the following procedures:

1. *Know where the person sank.* Watch the distressed person's exact location throughout your rescue swim. When you can, use spotters to pinpoint the location. If you can, include a marker buoy with your rescue equipment so you can mark the last known location of the victim.

2. *If you have to search for the person, search in an organized, rather than random, manner.* Time is of the essence, so use it wisely. Enlist the aid of teams of scuba divers to help search.

3. *Don't be fooled by a current.* Rescuers usually find victims almost directly below the point where they sank, even in moderately strong currents. Starting a search downcurrent may waste valuable time.

4. *When you locate a casualty, be sure he really is unconscious.* Grab the person and shake him to check for response.

5. *Quickly survey the person and his surroundings.* Check to see if the person is entangled in anything. Examine the person's face, scuba unit, and weight system. If the scuba regulator is in the person's mouth, leave it in. If the regulator is not in the person's mouth, do not waste time trying to reinsert it. If the person's mask is empty or filled with water, leave it be, but remove a partially flooded mask because air expanding inside the mask during ascent will force water in the mask into the person through the nose.

6. *Make the victim buoyant using the techniques described in the previous section.* If you cannot make the victim buoyant, make yourself buoyant and grasp the distressed diver tightly.

7. *To surface a breathing, unconscious diver, bring the diver upright, position yourself behind him, hold his regulator in place, hold his head in an upright, neutral position, and ascend.*

8. *When surfacing a nonbreathing diver, just get him to the surface (see figure 7.15).* Do not concern yourself with the position of his head. An unconscious diver cannot experience a lung overexpansion injury because his glottis relaxes after loss of consciousness. It is difficult to get air into an unconscious person, but it escapes freely regardless of head position. If you tilt a person's head back during your ascent, you allow water to pour into the person's lungs. It is a waste of time to surface an unconscious diver feet first.

9. *As you approach the surface, the person's buoyancy may increase.* You can control the rate of ascent by maneuvering the distressed diver into a horizontal, face-down position. The increased cross-sectional area increases resistance to motion and slows your rate of ascent. If you have time, examine and release the person's scuba equipment straps while you ascend. Turn the victim to a face-up position as you reach the surface.

10. *Unless your decompression status places you at risk, do not concern yourself about the rate of ascent.* Your priority is to get the victim to the surface. Don't worry about the person suffering decompression sickness. You can get people treated for bends, but they will die within a few minutes without air. If decompression sickness is a personal concern, release the buoyant victim while you ascend at the correct rate. Someone at the surface may be able to attend to the victim until you surface. If you position the person face up, he may begin breathing at the surface. You do not have to endanger yourself to save someone.

You must use a different procedure when a diver is experiencing seizures while submerged. The victim's throat is locked shut during the seizure. Taking or sending the victim to the surface before the seizure subsides will likely cause the person's lungs to rupture. If the victim's mask and mouthpiece are in place, leave them there. Be sure that the regulator mouthpiece does not fall out when the convulsions subside. If breathing resumes after the seizure, swim the victim to the surface while holding the mouthpiece

Figure 7.15 Learn how to locate and surface an unconscious diver.

in place. If the victim does not resume breathing after the seizure, proceed as described previously for an unconscious diver. The victim may lose the mouthpiece before convulsing. For this situation you should position the victim face down and wait for the convulsions to subside. As soon as the victim stops convulsing, attempt to insert the scuba regulator mouthpiece into the victim's mouth. The victim will begin breathing spontaneously after the seizure. Your goal is to ensure that the victim breathes air instead of water. Do not attempt to insert the mouthpiece during convulsions. You will not be successful, and you could be bitten severely.

Opening the Airway

Your second diving rescue goal is to ensure that the person is breathing when you reach the surface. If you can hear and see the person breathing, all you have to do is assist the individual. If the person is not breathing, you must act immediately to ensure respiration. Frequently all you need to do to allow an unconscious person to breathe is to open the person's airway. Merely tilting the person's head back may not suffice. You should support the jaw to help lift the tongue from the back of the person's throat (American Heart Association 2000). Supporting a casualty's jaw while you are in the water is not easy. The most effective technique is the head-tilt/jaw-thrust method shown in figure 7.16. Place your ring and middle fingers of both hands beneath the person's jaw and tilt the head back while lifting upward on the jaw bone.

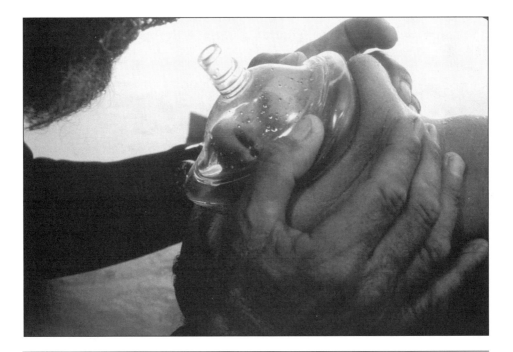

Figure 7.16 Whenever possible, use the head-tilt/jaw-thrust method to open the airway.

Rescue Breathing

You must ventilate a nonbreathing person. Several methods of aquatic artificial respiration—rescue breathing—are available. You should be familiar with various techniques because you may have to use different methods for different conditions. You may also have to use a combination of rescue breathing techniques. The more techniques you can master, the better prepared you will be to save a life.

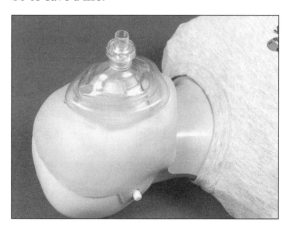

Figure 7.17 Close-up of a rescue breathing mask, which allows aquatic rescue breathing that is superior to all other forms of expired-air artificial respiration.

The best possible technique is one that I discovered during a diver rescue workshop in Hawaii. A rescuer can administer effective rescue breathing with a rescue breathing mask, which is available from many manufacturers. The mask technique maintains a correct airway with jaw lift, helps keep water out of the victim, ventilates the victim through both mouth and nose, eliminates mouth-to-mouth contact with the victim, and allows the rescuer to swim effectively. Both swimmers and divers may use the technique. Figure 7.17 depicts the rescue breathing mask and the rescue breathing technique.

RESCUE MASK BREATHING (HOW TO DO IT)

A rescue breathing mask eliminates direct contact with a casualty's mouth and nose, permits mouth-plus-nose rescue breathing, permits use of the triple-airway maneuver (head tilt, jaw thrust, opening mouth), and allows oxygen first aid for breathing or nonbreathing victims.

There are three in-water mask breathing techniques and three techniques for land use. The first step for each method is to prepare the mask for use. Push your thumbs into the folded mask and extend the dome. Attach the one-way valve to the mask inlet tube if you choose to use the valve to minimize disease transmission.

The second step is to open the person's airway and position the mask on the person's face. Place the wide end of the mask between the person's chin and lower lip with the pointed end of the mask covering the nose. Use the mask to retract the person's lower lip so the mouth remains open under the mask. On a person who has a small face, you may reverse the mask (pointed end on or under the chin). Open the airway and seal the mask by placing your index, middle, and ring fingers of both hands behind the angles of the jaw in front of the ear lobes and pull upward to position the lower teeth in front of the upper teeth. At the same time, clamp the mask sides with both thumbs to act like C clamps and tilt the person's head backward. If the person is prone, the most comfortable position for the rescuer is lying down and supported by the elbows.

The final step is to exhale into the mouthpiece of the mask 12 to 16 times per minute to ventilate a nonbreathing victim. On masks equipped with an oxygen inlet nipple, oxygen-enriched rescue breathing is possible by connecting an oxygen supply hose to the nipple. Once the victim's lungs inflate, remove your mouth from the mask and let the person's exhalations exit through the mouthpiece hole. Intermittently occluding the mask port with the lips after the person exhales increases oxygen concentrations when the oxygen flow rate is 25 liters per minute (lpm) or higher.

The first (and preferred) method of aquatic rescue breathing using a mask is the two-handed C-clamp technique (see figure 7.18a). The rescuer can maintain a good airway; see, hear, and tow the person well; and ventilate the person effectively even in choppy water. A properly sealed mask allows a victim's face to be submerged without consequence during rescue breathing. Both swimming and diving rescuers can use this technique effectively.

The second method of mask rescue breathing is the buoyant chin-lift method (see figure 7.18b). You will need flotation for elevation above the victim. Clamp the chin-end of the mask with the thumb on the skirt of the mask and two fingers on the bony part under the chin. Lift upward with your fingers. Avoid pressing your fingers into the fleshy part of the chin because you could restrict the airway. Clamp the upper end of the mask with your thumb and forefinger on the mask skirt and the remainder of your hand pressing downward on the person's forehead.

The third, and least desirable, mask technique for aquatic rescue breathing is the neck-lift procedure in which you are beside and at the same level as the victim (see figure 7.18c). Position the mask on the person's face with the thumb and fingers of one hand and press downward to seal the mask and tilt the head backward. Lift upward on the back of the person's neck with the other hand. You will need fins to use this technique effectively.

On land, use the two-handed C-clamp technique to seal the mask and open the airway. When possible, attach an oxygen tube to the mask. A lone rescuer who must perform CPR alongside the victim may use the chin-lift technique.

Disadvantages of the rescue mask technique are that you must have a mask and you must know how to use it. You can carry a rescue mask in the pocket of your BCD or tucked inside your bathing suit. Obtain rescue masks through your local fire department. Everyone should have a rescue breathing mask and keep it close at hand for any emergency that may require artificial respiration.

Another rescue breathing technique is mouth-to-snorkel. The late Albert Pierce (1985), a diving instructor, rescue expert, and good friend, promoted the technique for many years. Mouth-to-snorkel is now a difficult procedure because of the complex nature of modern equipment, but it qualified as an effective technique when snorkels were simple tubes. The procedure could allow a rescuer to maintain a correct airway with jaw lift, keep the victim's airway dry, eliminate mouth-to-mouth contact with the victim, and allow the rescuer to swim effectively. Both swimmers and divers with snorkels could use the technique. Most modern snorkels are not useful for mouth-to-snorkel rescue breathing because they have exhaust valves and water exclusion devices that will not permit use of the technique. Figure 7.19 shows the mouth-to-snorkel rescue breathing technique.

a

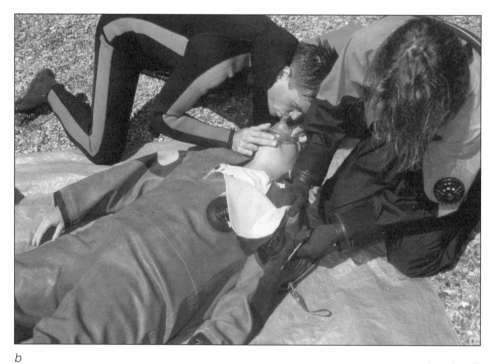

b

(continued)

Figure 7.18 Aquatic rescue breathing techniques include the *(a)* C-clamp method, the *(b)* chin-lift method which can be used in the water as well as on land, and the *(c)* neck-lift method, which is the least desirable of the three.

c

Figure 7.18 *(continued)*

Figure 7.19 Mouth-to-snorkel can be an effective rescue breathing technique if you have the right snorkel type and are proficient with the procedure.

Figure 7.20 Buoyant chin-lift rescue breathing can be effective in calm water when you can make a victim buoyant and when you have floatation to lift yourself above the person in distress.

A third method of rescue breathing that incorporates the important jaw positioning is the buoyant chin-lift technique. You may use the technique when you can make a victim buoyant and when you have a float to lift yourself above the distressed diver as illustrated in figure 7.20. The procedure is the same as that for mouth-to-mouth artificial respiration on land.

Buoyant chin-lift rescue breathing does not work well if you cannot make a casualty buoyant or if the water is rough. You must have a suitable float to lift yourself above the person in distress. You cannot kick well to transport a victim. This procedure is the same as that for mouth-to-mask artificial respiration on land.

Thousands of divers have learned the "do-si-do" method of in-water artificial respiration shown in figure 7.21. The arm-in-arm method is similar to the do-si-do square dance position. While some situations, such as rough water, require that you use the do-si-do technique, it should *not* be your first choice as a rescue breathing technique. The following list identifies the disadvantages of the do-si-do technique.

- Lack of jaw lift. Failure to lift the jaw may not maintain an open airway and may allow ventilated air to go into the victim's stomach instead of the lungs.

- Water may flow into the victim's mouth and nose, especially in choppy water.

- The rescuer's kick is not as effective as it is when the rescuer is ahead of a victim (as with the rescue breathing mask or snorkel breathing techniques).

Figure 7.21 You should know how to administer mouth-to-mouth rescue breathing, but it should not be your first choice because it has several disadvantages. Here the author demonstrates the do-si-do technique by blowing on the victim's cheek.

- The rescuer has mouth-to-mouth contact with the nonbreathing person.
- The technique is extremely difficult for a rescuer without fins.

Another method of mouth-to-mouth rescue breathing you can use when you do not have adjunct breathing aids or a float is the neck-lift technique described in table 7.2. Use the procedure when you find it difficult to get close enough to ventilate someone or when a victim lacks buoyancy. The disadvantages of the procedure are the same as those for the do-si-do method.

Table 7.2   Aquatic Rescue Breathing Comparisons

Method	Chin lift for optimum airway
Mouth-to-mouth do-si-do	Poor
Mouth-to-mouth neck-lift	Poor
Mouth-to-mouth buoyant chin-lift	Excellent
Mouth-to-nose	Poor
Mouth-to-snorkel	Fair
Mouth-to-mask (from one side)	Poor
Mouth-to-mask (center line)	Excellent
Mouth-to-mask buoyant chin-lift	Excellent

When you cannot administer mask or mouth-to-snorkel rescue breathing and the water is too rough for mouth-to-mouth to be effective, try mouth-to-nose rescue breathing. You can keep a victim drier than with mouth-to-mouth, although the other disadvantages of mouth-to-mouth still apply.

The ABCDE of Rescue Breathing

Use the ABCDE procedure when you initiate any form of rescue breathing in the water.

A. Open the victim's **A**irway (using the chin lift, if possible).

B. Put your cheek and ear close to the person's mouth, and watch his chest while you look, listen, and feel for **B**reathing.

C. If a victim is not breathing, remove his mask while **C**alling for help. You may or may not remove your mask depending on its size and on water conditions. Rescue breathing is easier if you can breathe through both your nose and mouth.

D. Turn the person's head to the side, pull down one corner of the person's mouth, and **D**rain any water from the mouth and throat. If you can open the person's mouth, do a finger sweep of the mouth.

E. **E**xhale two full breaths into the victim to initiate rescue breathing. If you cannot ventilate a nonbreathing person, reposition the airway and try again. If you are unsuccessful, position yourself beneath the person, perform a Heimlich maneuver, and reattempt ventilations. After you initiate ventilations, continue at the rate of two ventilations every 10 seconds. For mouth-to-mouth or mouth-to-nose techniques, roll the injured person's body (not head) slightly toward you to reduce the effort required to lift yourself in the water. Anytime water enters the person's airway, drain the water before giving additional ventilations.

Rescue breathing suggestions:

1. Expect foam to come from the victim's mouth and nose. Water in the lungs causes surfactant, a surface tension-reducing agent produced by the body, to foam.

2. Do not be alarmed if you cannot open a victim's mouth at first. Oxygen deprivation can cause seizures, which may lock the jaw temporarily. Ventilate the person using the rescue breathing mask or mouth-to-nose technique until the person's jaw muscles relax.

3. Conserve as much energy as possible. Lift yourself upward only when you ventilate a person. Keep yourself low in the water when you are not ventilating.

4. Watch the water while you ventilate a person. Note the direction of any chop, waves, or current. Position your back to rough water to shield the person. Look where you want to go and take the most direct route.

5. Learn to ventilate a victim from either side. You won't have to delay initiation of rescue breathing if you find yourself on the wrong side of an injured diver, and you will find it helpful to be able to switch sides while removing an injured diver's equipment.

Equipment Removal

You need to remove equipment when you rescue a scuba diver. How much you remove from yourself and a victim and when you remove the equipment varies with circumstances. You should discard the distressed person's weights at the outset of a rescue. You should probably remove your weights when you have a victim at the surface, although some rescuers with thick exposure suits prefer to retain the weights so they can remain upright and in control. Some divers wear two weight belts so they can discard a portion of their weight for buoyancy and still maintain control (Graver 1995). Remove the victim's mask if you have to administer rescue breathing. Except for rough water conditions, remove your mask to perform rescue breathing. If you have to transport a victim more than 25 yards, remove scuba equipment from yourself and the person in distress.

In an actual emergency do not concern yourself about lost equipment. Your priority is to expedite the rescue. Do not worry about the equipment until after the emergency. When you practice rescue techniques, however, take measures to prevent equipment loss. Use equipment handlers and carefully pass the equipment to them instead of discarding it.

Become familiar with various types of equipment releases. Learn how to release weights and scuba units. Practice removing equipment from a person simulating an unconscious diver. You need to know what to remove, when to remove it, and how to remove it. Use a commonsense approach to decide what to remove and when (e.g., do not remove the scuba unit from a tropical diver who does not have an exposure suit because you will remove the person's only source of buoyancy).

Work slowly and deliberately while you remove equipment. Quick, forceful movements literally make waves that can flood a victim's airway. Avoid reaching across a diver's face to unfasten equipment because water draining from your arm may run into the person's mouth and nose. Continue ventilations during equipment removal. Give the injured person two breaths, take up to nine seconds to work on the equipment, then prepare to give the person two more breaths by the tenth second. You are likely to rush ventilations unless you time your breaths. Count to yourself: one-one thousand, two-one thousand, three-one thousand, and so on. Do not feel that you have to complete the removal of an item of equipment during a single ventilation interval. Use multiple intervals and you will do a better job.

Here is a general, sequential approach for equipment removal when both you and the victim have exposure suits and scuba equipment:

1. Remove the victim's weights.
2. Remove your weights.

3. Remove the victim's mask.

4. Remove your mask (except in rough water conditions).

5. Remove your scuba equipment (you have to lift it during ventilations).

6. Remove the victim's scuba equipment (unless the victim lacks buoyancy).

7. Remove your fins before a shallow-water exit.

When you remove an injured diver's mask, especially for practice, lift the part of the mask that covers the nose before you pull the mask from the person (this is less painful for the person simulating a victim!). You will find it easier to remove your scuba equipment if you vent the air from your BCD first. Removal of a victim's scuba unit can be difficult if the person is using an older jacket-type BCD that lacks quick-disconnect fasteners at the shoulders. Try pulling the person's arm through the armhole hand first. If unsuccessful with the hand-pull method, try deflating the flotation device and pushing it down one arm of the victim with one hand while pulling the victim's arm—elbow first—through the armhole with your other hand. Avoid fighting with the equipment to remove it. Postpone removal of a troublesome item until you reach shallow water or until you obtain assistance. Equipment removal obviously is easier when you have someone to assist you. Practice rescue techniques unassisted, however, because you may not have help during a scuba rescue. Ask role-playing victims to give you objective feedback about airway positioning, water exclusion, and the ventilation rate.

Before you practice rescue techniques, inform lifeguards and other people in the area that you will be practicing skills. Have those playing the role of victims indicate that all is well by displaying an OK sign during practice (see figure 7.22).

Figure 7.22 Have a "victim" signal he or she is OK during practice sessions.

Victim Transport

After you establish buoyancy, initiate rescue breathing, and remove equipment as needed, your next task is to transport the victim to boat or shore while continuing rescue breathing. Pace yourself so you will have sufficient energy for the endeavor. Whenever possible, get others to help you. Your job will be easier when you can have someone push or pull the victim while you concentrate on rescue breathing. Look around while you transport someone. You may be able to signal and stop a passing boat and get the victim out of the water quickly.

For boat-based rescue situations, try to use a line for assistance. Take a line with you when you go to the aid of a distressed diver. Many dive boats trail a line from the stern (back) of the boat to aid divers returning to the boat against any current. Look for a trail line. The trail line may be closer to you than the vessel. If so, transport the victim to the trail line, hold onto the line and the person in distress, and have someone on the boat pull you to the vessel. Instruct the person on the boat to pull gently so as not to pull the line from your grasp (see figure 7.23). The resistance of two people moving through the water is strong.

Boat-based diving victims often get into trouble down current from the boat. They exhaust themselves trying to swim against the current to get back to the boat. You may find it difficult or impossible to make progress against the current during a rescue. Someone on the boat may be able to float a line to you while you work against the flow. Fighting a current is futile. If you can't transport a victim against the current, tell someone aboard the boat to bring the vessel to you.

When you transport a victim to shore, it helps to know the shoreline. Pick the best point for your landing and swim directly to it. Compensate for any current.

Figure 7.23 Practice retrieving a victim with the aid of a line. The person pulling the line should do so slowly and easily.

You may need to swim at an angle to a current to reach the desired location. As you approach shore, look for people to help you. Tell them to throw you a line or wade in and help you get a victim out of the water. Transporting an injured diver through a surf zone effectively is particularly difficult, requires special training and frequent practice, and is something to avoid unless you know the procedures or you have no choice.

Rescue Exits

The exit is the most difficult part of a diver rescue. You are tired, the victim is heavy, and the situation may require significant effort. Enlist aid whenever possible. Use the easiest possible technique for the circumstances. Do your best to continue ventilations during the exit.

There are many rescue exit techniques because there are numerous exit situations. You may have to exit onto a boat, shore, or dock. The water at the exit point may be deep or shallow, rough or calm. The bottom conditions may be smooth or rocky. You may or may not have assistance. As with all aspects of diver rescue, you should know a variety of techniques for different circumstances.

If possible, keep a victim in a horizontal position during the exit. If a diver has suffered an air embolism, bubbles lodged in arteries to the brain may move and produce serious consequences when you shift the injured person to a vertical position. Whenever you can, select a rescue exit that keeps the person's body as level as possible.

Figure 7.24 depicts an effective boat rescue exit. You may be able to direct the exit procedures while you continue rescue breathing in the water. Avoid a prolonged interruption of ventilations. Agree on a plan of action before you relinquish the victim to well-meaning people who may not care for the injured person correctly.

Without help, you may not be able to get a person into a boat. If you find yourself in such a plight, use the boat for surface support and continue to ventilate the injured diver until you can summon aid or until you no longer have the strength to continue. A loop of line draped over the side of an anchored boat has many uses: support for rescue breathing, support for scuba equipment when exiting the water, and a stirrup for assistance in boarding the vessel.

Shore rescue techniques also vary. You may be able to float a victim to the water's edge. When footing will be poor, you need to float a person as far as possible. You can then lift the injured person into a sitting position, grasp him under the arms, and drag him out of the water. Be sure to keep your back straight and use your legs for lifting. You can move a person much larger than yourself by repeatedly straightening your legs and falling backwards into a sitting position. Use the three-person carry depicted in figure 7.25 when you can get someone to assist you. Instruct helpers. Tell them what you want done and how to do it.

You may find yourself in a situation in which you have no choice but to take a victim through surf unassisted. First get rid of all equipment except exposure

Figure 7.24 Learn and practice several boat rescue exit techniques. Be prepared to organize and direct the exits.

suits and fins. Pause outside the surf zone, evaluate the conditions, and time the waves. Waves commonly occur in sets with periods of large waves followed by periods of smaller waves (Graver 1999). Try to make your exit coincide with a period of small waves. Use the do-si-do position for control and grasp the victim firmly. Cover the injured person's mouth and nose when water washes over the individual's face. A rescue breathing mask held over a nonbreathing person's mouth and nose protects the person well in rough water. Allow the waves to carry you toward shore while you lift the person as high as possible. Brace against the backrush, which has a tendency to turn the victim parallel to incoming waves. If a wave tumbles you and tears a victim from your grasp, recover as quickly as possible, regain contact with the helpless individual, and proceed. Attempt to ventilate a victim between waves. Remember to drain any water from the nonbreathing person's mouth before you ventilate. If you need to do a surf rescue exit, learn and practice the techniques before you need to use them.

Practice rescue exits in a variety of settings. Identify effective techniques for sites you visit frequently. Practice with someone simulating an unconscious victim until rescue exits are easy to manage. Vividly imagining rescue procedures can be helpful, but hands-on experience is the best way to prepare yourself for an actual rescue.

Self-Rescue Techniques

Part of being a prepared rescuer is to be prepared to rescue yourself if circumstances require. Have an alternate source of air in addition to your primary scuba unit. The deeper you dive, the more important it is to have an alternate source

Figure 7.25 Learn a variety of shore exit techniques.

of air. A nearby buddy can supply air, but don't rely on your buddy for air in an emergency. Consider one of several types of redundant scuba systems.

Rebreathing air from your BCD is another viable option for self-preservation (see figure 7.26). You use exhaled air for artificial respiration, so you may rebreathe it. The stimulation of stretch receptors in your chest also partially relieves air hunger. Additionally, BCD rebreathing allows you to breathe fresh air you added to the BCD for buoyancy control. This can extend the duration of a small supply of air in your scuba tank. Learn the BCD rebreathing technique, then reserve it for emergencies. You could develop a lung infection by breathing air from a BCD, but you would be willing to take that risk if you were about to drown. The following are the procedures for rebreathing air from a BCD. Practice the procedure in shallow water before attempting the technique in deep water. As a safety precaution, have someone observe you. Before you practice, disinfect your BCD with a diluted solution of Zephiran Chloride, available at many drugstores.

1. Lift the BCD hose to a vertical position and hold it there for several seconds to allow any water inside to drain into the BCD.

2. Place the BCD mouthpiece in your mouth.

3. Begin exhaling and almost immediately thereafter depress the manual inflation button on the BCD control valve. The reason you exhale briefly before depressing the button is to expel the water inside the mouthpiece through a nonreturn valve. Keep the valve button depressed firmly and continuously. If you release the button, you will have to clear the mouthpiece again.

Figure 7.26 You should learn to rebreathe air from your BCD so you can use the procedure as an underwater emergency option.

4. Exhale about half your remaining air into the BCD, keep the BCD valve depressed, then rebreathe the air. Inhale cautiously so you will not inspire droplets of water from the BCD hose or mouthpiece. Place the tip of your tongue on the roof of your mouth to divert any water droplets you may draw into your mouth. If you choke on a drop of water, cough into the BCD so you won't lose air.

5. As you ascend, surrounding pressure decreases and the volume of the air inside your BCD increases. Exhale air through your nose to avoid excessive buoyancy.

Make yourself buoyant if you are scuba diving and believe you are about to drown. You must act deliberately before your behavior becomes instinctive. If the situation is serious and you begin losing control, remove your weights and hold them close to you with one hand. If you do lose control of your actions or lose consciousness, you will drop the weights and become buoyant.

Rescue Preparedness

The chances of a successful scuba rescue increase in proportion to your preparation. The following areas of recommendations are for all divers and those who may be in a position to rescue scuba divers:

1. Be trained in first aid, CPR, scuba diving, and scuba rescue techniques.

2. Become familiar with scuba diving equipment, especially weighting systems and scuba units.

3. Obtain and have available various items of rescue equipment.

4. Obtain and have available local emergency contact information. Know who to call for scuba diving emergencies and how to place the call.

5. Practice self-rescue and rescue techniques periodically to maintain proficiency.

6. Determine the emergency qualifications, if any, of people present at a dive site. Develop and agree on an emergency plan of action.

7. Decide in advance that if you can safely manage an emergency, you will take action.

Key Points

Scuba diving is much different from swimming, so rescuing scuba divers is different from rescuing swimmers. Scuba rescues require more knowledge, training, and equipment than swimmer rescues. You need to learn what to look for, how to prepare for and respond to a scuba diving rescue, and how to perform all of the skills that may be needed to save the life of a scuba diver.

Chapter **8**

Watercraft-Related Submersion Injuries

An individual in water may be injured, but when a watercraft becomes part of the situation, injury types increase and rescues become more complicated. Victims may be burned; have broken bones, deep lacerations, head injuries, or internal bleeding; and may be entrapped or entangled. There may be multiple victims. Incidents may occur far from shore.

A **SCUBA DIVER WAS SURFACING FROM A DIVE** at Catalina Island 26 miles offshore from California. A cabin cruiser was proceeding toward the island at a slow speed of five knots. The vessel ran over the diver just as he surfaced. The boat propeller inflicted numerous deep cuts to the man's back and shoulder. I was employed to investigate the accident and learned some frightening information.

I attached a line to the bottom and tethered myself five feet from the surface. I had the boat that struck the victim pass directly over me at a speed of five knots while I photographed the vessel. The water visibility was excellent—about 75 to 80 feet horizontally. I was surprised to discover that I was unable to hear the boat approaching. I could not hear the sound of the engine until the vessel was directly above me and after it had passed me. A scuba diver surfacing in the path of a moving vessel is in great danger. The proper use of dive flags is important and was underscored for me during my investigation.

Learning Goals *By the end of this chapter, you should be able to:*

▶ List three potential causes of death from propeller injuries.

▶ State two actions that are most likely to reduce boating fatalities.

▶ List the three most frequent causes of boating fatalities.

▶ Describe the relationship between alcohol consumption and boating accidents.

▶ List four common sources of entanglement that cause boating submersion injuries.

▶ Describe the potential hazard posed by low head dams.

▶ List various approved and nonapproved boating distress signals.

▶ List 8 of 10 items of rescue equipment recommended for all vessels.

▶ List 7 of 9 items of equipment recommended for rescue swimmers.

▶ Explain how to approach boating accident situations in a rescue vessel.

▶ Describe the roles of personnel aboard a rescue vessel.

Propeller injuries are just one cause of watercraft-related submersion injuries. Stop Propeller Injuries Now (SPIN), a group dedicated to the reduction of these injuries, strongly encourages the use of propeller guards. If a propeller injury does not cause a victim to drown, severe blood loss may cause rapid death from shock. If the victim survives the initial trauma, infection caused by contaminated water being sucked into veins may lead to amputation and even death.

More than 13 million vessels are registered in the United States. Boating fatalities averaged 788 per year for the years 1994 through 1999. There were 734 deaths from 7, 931 reported boating accidents in 1999 (National Safety Council 2001). Table 8.1 lists the types of watercraft and activities involved in fatal accidents in 1999.

The National Safety Council (2001) reported that 72 percent of all boating fatalities in 1997 were due to drowning and that 89 percent of the victims were not wearing personal flotation devices. If you knew that 9 out of 10 boating deaths occurred to boaters who did not wear flotation devices, you probably would be inclined to wear a personal flotation device every time you board a

Table 8.1 Fatalities Involving Watercraft and Water Activities

Vessel type	1999 fatalities	Activity	1999 fatalities
Open boat	408	Fishing	181
Canoes/kayaks	84	Racing	2
Personal watercraft	66	Repairs	12
Rowboats	50	Skiing/tubing	22
Cabin cruisers	46	Whitewater	25
Sail only	5	Starting engine	1
Auxiliary sail	14	Hunting	13
Pontoon	20	Unreported	463
Inflatable	14	Other	9
Houseboats	14		
Other	12		

vessel. The next time you have the opportunity to observe boaters, take note of how many people are uninformed. The National Safety Council (2001) also reported that in 95 percent of boating fatalities the operator had no known boater education. This statistic supports the old adage that what you don't know can kill you.

Fatality Causes

Capsizing, falling overboard, and collisions are the three most frequent causes of boating injuries and deaths. Other causes, from most frequent to least frequent, include flooding and swamping, sinking, skier accidents, grounding, being struck by a vessel, fire or explosion, and falls aboard vessels. The important point of these statistics is that the great majority involve the victim being in the water (National Safety Council 2001).

Although not being listed as a cause, bad weather or sudden changes in weather and sea conditions must be considered because they contribute to capsizing, flooding, swamping, sinking, and people falling overboard. Having been involved with marine rescues for many years, I am firmly convinced that the number of boating accidents and fatalities would be only a small percentage of the current figures if watercraft operators avoided poor boating conditions.

I **T WAS 9:30 P.M. ON A CHILLY FALL EVENING** in the Pacific Northwest. A wind that developed suddenly made the air temperature feel colder than it actually was. My firefighter turnout gear felt good as I stepped from our aid unit into the buffeting wind. My crew and I were responding to a call about boaters in the Puget Sound waters at Camano Island, Washington. A homeowner along the shore had heard cries for help and phoned 911. The reporting party told us that he had seen several people clinging to an overturned boat and that the boat had disappeared around a point on the island. We found some steps on a bluff and made our way to the beach. After wading along the shore through overhead tree branches for about 100 yards, we found four men and a small boy exiting the water. We covered them with blankets and took them to our aid units, where we treated them for hypothermia. They were victims of the sudden wind. None of them were wearing personal flotation devices. I wanted to ask them why they were out in a small boat in the dark with a four-year-old child and no flotation devices, but I held my tongue. Our job is to treat people, not to challenge their wisdom. If this incident had occurred farther from shore, there could easily have been five fatalities. The incident could have been avoided completely if the boaters had checked the weather forecast before their adventure.

Alcohol is another factor that leads to accidents. Alcohol consumption is a factor in more than half of all watercraft accidents (National Transportation Safety Board 1993). As little as one alcoholic drink or beverage can affect a person's judgment and reaction time. There is no doubt that avoidance of alcohol would greatly lower boating fatality statistics.

Boating accidents occur when children and adolescents operate watercraft. Seventeen states do not have laws for minimum operator age; only one state has a minimum age of 18. The most common minimum operator age is 12, which most would agree is too young. Common sense should prevail over the law's minimum requirements. Swift, powerful vessels can be weapons in the hands of the young and inexperienced. Parents should not allow youth to operate watercraft.

Entrapment occurs when boats overturn. People trapped inside a capsized vessel in rough water are disoriented and in complete blackness. Panic occurs rapidly. Another type of vessel entrapment occurs when a person is beneath an overturned vessel.

I WILL NEVER FORGET TRYING TO LAUNCH AN INFLATABLE BOAT through the surf in California. A wave much larger than any preceding it lifted the bow of the boat straight up and flipped it over on top of me. As I struggled to get my head above water, I bumped into the boat, which was moving toward shore with the wave. I pushed up on the boat and tried to duck my head beneath the pontoon to get out from beneath the craft, but I could not because I was trying to get out on the side that was toward shore. I fought the urge to panic, thought about what was happening, and allowed the boat to move above me until I felt the opposite pontoon. I was then able to push up on the boat, duck my head beneath the pontoon, and free myself. I surfaced to see the boat surfing toward shore in the wave and a friend of mine, who was waiting on the beach, doubled over with laughter. I did not tell him that I had nearly reached the breaking point for both breath holding and emotional control. I could have died if I had stopped thinking. It is a particularly scary feeling to be trapped underwater.

Entanglement causes submersion injuries. Boaters get tangled in anchor lines, trap lines, and other lines and fall overboard. When a boat breaks apart during a collision, exposed wires and cables are another source of entanglement. Scuba divers diving from boats may become entangled in kelp. Boats anchored in the wind swing from side to side on the anchor line. The stronger the wind, the wider the arc of the swing.

ON A WINDY DAY IN THE 1980s, a scuba diver entered the water from a California charter boat and became tangled in the kelp. The diver was pushed beneath the surface when the boat, which was swinging on the anchor line, swept over him. The diver drowned because his scuba regulator—his air supply—was trapped behind in the kelp. The scuba diver was taught to enter the water with the regulator in his mouth, but he did not apply his training. Life support equipment will not preserve you if you do not use it properly.

The true causes of boating accidents are not reflected in the statistical charts for fatalities. The charts list capsizing, flooding, swamping, grounding, and sinking as causes; they do not identify why these events occurred. One of the primary reasons boaters get into serious trouble is the combination of poor mechanical maintenance and rough water conditions. A moving boat is less likely to swamp than one that sits helplessly. A boat without power that drifts into shallow water will broach (turn sideways) and get swamped by the waves that form when the water depth decreases. A boat that will not start when a sudden wind makes the water rough is a vessel likely to get into trouble. Loss of steerage also places a vessel in jeopardy. Boats must be well maintained to avoid becoming at the mercy of the wind and waves.

Poor planning and inattentiveness that lead to running out of fuel place boaters in the same predicament as lack of mechanical maintenance. A good boater knows how much fuel will be needed for the excursion and ensures that more than enough fuel is aboard.

Overloaded vessels are prone to swamping, flooding, and sinking. When you see a boat full of people with only a couple of inches of the boat above the surface of the water, expect trouble. The wake from a passing boat is sufficient to swamp and sink the overloaded vessel. Boats are required to have weight capacity placards, but these safety aids are of no use if they are ignored. Unfortunately, overloading is a common problem.

Water skiing accidents are included in boating accident statistics. There are rules and equipment to minimize the dangers of water skiing. Adhering to the rules decreases the chances of a serious accident, while ignoring the rules and omitting safety equipment increases the odds that someone will be injured or killed.

Another cause of boating accidents does not occur often, but it is definitely noteworthy. Years ago at an aquatic conference I watched a film produced by the Lutheran Brotherhood about low head dams. When water drops over a low head dam, which may be only a foot in height, a circular current is produced called a hydraulic. The hydraulic is a powerful downward current near the dam. The film documented an attempted rescue of two boaters whose vessel was swamped by the hydraulic. A rescue vessel slowly approached the dam to assist the boaters, who surfaced briefly and disappeared again repeatedly. When the rescue boat was a few feet from the dam, it was pulled forward suddenly and sucked down into the hydraulic. The rescuers became victims. The area in the vicinity of low head dams must be avoided.

Types of Injuries

Boating-related injuries often involve factors that differ from those involved in swimming injuries. A fire, explosion, or fall from a boat may cause a boater in the water to be burned or have broken bones or internal injuries. The combination of trauma and hypothermia is wretched. While either one may not be sufficient to cause death, the synergetic effect of them can be fatal rapidly because burned and injured victims become hypothermic much faster than those who are uninjured. Fuel, which may be present in the water after a collision, can cause chemical burns and inhalation poisoning.

Head injuries that may cause spinal cord damage may be more common in boating accidents than in swimming accidents. Victims may hit their heads when they fall inside or out of a vessel. Victims in the water, including water skiers, scuba divers, and swimmers, may be struck by watercraft. The shifting boom of a sailboat may strike a sailor. Whitewater rafters and kayakers may hit their heads on rocks when tossed from their vessels or adrift in churning, swift-moving water. Always consider the possibility of head and spinal cord injuries when rescuing the victims of watercraft accidents.

Recognition

A good way to recognize watercraft emergencies is to use your powers of observation to predict them. Watch boaters at marinas, docks, and boat launching ramps. Boats that are difficult to start, overloaded, or poorly maintained are easy to spot. Pay attention to these vessels and those aboard them because you may be called on to lend assistance to their occupants before your outing is completed.

Another way to spot accidents waiting to happen is to know the forecasts for weather and water conditions. Check the weather conditions on a marine weather radio (162.4 MHz), the tide and current charts, and the barometer before venturing out on the water. Many boaters just look out the window and go boating if the skies look good at the time. Conditions on the water can deteriorate quickly from good to terrible. If you see people operating vessels when you know that conditions are about to change, you won't be surprised if some of them get into trouble. It is a good idea to monitor emergency radio frequencies whenever you are boating. Calls for assistance may happen at any time. Listen to the radio traffic and respond to calls for help from distressed boaters in your area.

Boats are required to carry visual distress signals. The types required vary with the body of water, the vessel length, and whether the vessel operates during the day, night, or both. Table 8.2 lists the approved minimum distress signal requirements as well as nonapproved, but widely recognized, nautical distress signals. These are also internationally accepted signals for distress while afloat. Binoculars can help you identify emergency situations and should be part of the equipment that you have aboard your boat.

Table 8.2   Distress Signals

Approved minimum visual distress signals		Nonapproved, but widely recognized, nautical distress signals
Signal	Operation	Signal
Three handheld red flares	Day or night use	An S.O.S signal (three shorts, three longs, three shorts—either visual or audible)
Pistol-projected parachute red flare	Day or night use	Slowly and repeatedly raising and lowering outstretched arms
Three aerial pyrotechnic red flares	Day or night use	Flames aboard a vessel (e.g., burning rags in a bucket)
Three floating orange smoke flares	Day use only	A flag flown upside down
Three handheld orange smoke flares	Day use only	An article of clothing attached to an oar or a mast
One 3′ × 3′ orange flag	Day use only	

Rescues

A typical rescue for a boating accident involves the use of another boat. Your first thought as a rescuer is to avoid succumbing to the same fate as the victims you are trying to assist. At times the weather and water conditions may be so bad that you would be foolish to attempt a rescue using the equipment that you have available. Be prepared to summon professional help that is better equipped for the task.

Boating-related emergencies divide into two categories: assists and rescues. Unless the conditions are hazardous, any boater can and should provide assistance to another vessel in distress. Examples of assists are providing fuel or jump-starts, towing, retrieving people from a sinking vessel, and lending equipment or tools. Rescues involve extricating victims from the water and range from simple to complex. Do what you can within reason, but realize that professionals should respond to complex situations. Avoid high-risk rescue attempts.

Boating assists and rescues range from a private boater providing assistance to a government agency rescue vessel staffed with trained and fully equipped rescue swimmers performing complex water-based rescues. Before you rush to render aid, ask yourself the following questions:

1. Is my vessel appropriate for the conditions?
2. Do I have the personnel, training, and experience necessary?
3. Do I have the rescue and first aid equipment that may be required?

If you are not prepared, trained, and equipped for a rescue, summon and wait for professional aid. Adding rescue equipment to your boat can increase the ease and effectiveness of the assistance that you may provide. Table 8.3 lists recommended items for having aboard to help other boaters in trouble. Private vessels are not likely to have all of the equipment recommended in table 8.3, but the

Table 8.3   Rescue Equipment

Recommended boating rescue equipment	Recommended items for rescuing swimmers
Radio	Exposure suit with hood, boots, and gloves
Binoculars	Swim fins and mask
Fire extinguisher	Tether line and harness
75 feet of rope (in throw bag)	Helmet
Rescue buoys (torpedo type)	Knife
Throwable flotation device	Waterproof light
Horizontal extrication means*	Wire cutters
Telescoping boat hook	Signaling devices: strobe light, mirror, whistle, inflatable tube buoy
Anchor and anchor line	Marker buoy
First aid equipment**	

*Horizontal extrication means are discussed further in chapter 5. **Detailed list of equipment can be found in appendix B.

Figure 8.1 A professional rescue vessel.

more rescue equipment available, the better. Professional rescue vessels should have all of the recommended rescue and first aid equipment (see figure 8.1).

Approaches

Use caution when you approach a boating emergency. There may be fuel, debris, victims, and submerged obstacles in the water. It is a good idea to stop and survey the situation before venturing into the immediate area of the emergency. Your approach depends on many factors. The general rule is to approach the scene upwind or up current, whichever is greater. Maintaining a position against the wind or water is easier when opposing it, and your boat will not be pushed into or over objects and victims in the water. Sometimes, however, you will need to approach from the downwind or down current direction. Use this technique when fuel or chemicals are present or when obstructions are present on the downwind side. Avoid drifting or backing into an area when approaching downwind. The preferred procedure is to drop anchor upwind from the scene and let out the anchor line to reach the rescue area as depicted in figure 8.2.

The usual procedure is to slow your vessel to a no-wake speed as you approach the emergency scene. Waves produced by your vessel can be detrimental.

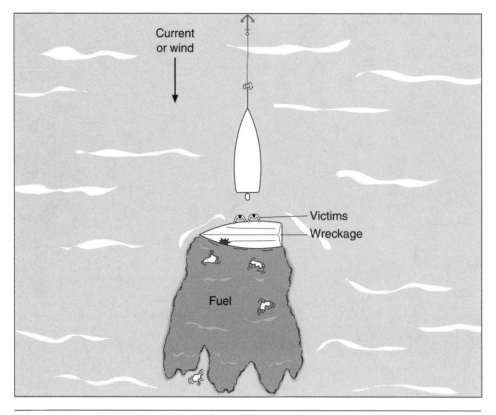

Figure 8.2 Anchor a rescue vessel upwind or upstream from a hazardous rescue area, and then let out the anchor line to approach the situation from the safe side.

On the other hand, a rough-water rescue technique that may be effective is to power a rescue vessel in a tight circle around a victim and rescue swimmer in the water to help flatten the surface.

Multiple victims are not uncommon in watercraft-related accidents. Assess the situation as you approach. Quickly provide buoyancy for the victims who are in the best condition and then rescue the person in the greatest need of assistance. Keep track of the remaining victims to avoid losing sight of them during the rescue of a victim.

Rescue Personnel and Operations

If you have to respond to a boating emergency alone, you won't be able to do much more than help victims into your vessel and transport them to safety and aid. Never leave your vessel unoccupied to assist a victim in the water. The wind can blow your boat out of reach, and you will become another victim.

Having at least one crew member for emergency response greatly increases your ability to provide assistance. The crew member can throw lines and floats,

Table 8.4   Jobs of Crew Members

Operator	First crew member	Second crew member	Third crew member
Global awareness	Lookout	Lookout and general helper	Primary rescue swimmer
Team leader	Swimmer tender	Rescue swimmer or backup	First aid provider
Radio communications	Readies rescue equipment	Helps ready primary swimmer	
Limited assistance to crew	Primary first aid provider	First aid provider	

extend a pole, grab a victim while you position the vessel, and more. Always try to take someone with you when you respond to a boating emergency.

The ideal situation is to have a trained crew of three or four who carry out a coordinated rescue. One person is the boat operator, who is in charge of the rescue team. The second crew member remains aboard the vessel. The third and fourth members are qualified rescue swimmers; one is designated as the primary swimmer and the other as the backup swimmer. The backup swimmer remains aboard the rescue boat unless needed in the water to assist the primary rescue swimmer. Table 8.4 lists the typical duties and tasks for the various personnel aboard a rescue vessel.

A rescue team must operate as a team—each member must know what the other will do. The team leader, who is the boat operator, has the greatest responsibility and needs to be aware of everything. Operating the vessel is only part of the team leader's duties. The leader must also take in the entire picture and make decisions that maximize safety for everyone involved. A qualified team leader's instructions must not be questioned in an emergency. There may not be time for discussion and debate. The leader must also communicate the status of rescues to various agencies. Crew members need to fulfill their responsibilities, work together, and keep the operator informed.

Key Points

Recreational boating is enjoyable, but it can be dangerous. Too many lives are lost unnecessarily because people fail to abide by simple safe boating rules. Rescue situations can be anticipated, and all boaters should be prepared and equipped to provide aid to other boaters in distress. In some situations, however, professional rescue assistance is the only feasible action. Have a means to summon assistance when a boating accident requires professional response.

Part IV

Emergency Procedures

Chapter 9

Photo courtesy of Ryan Shaughnessy

First Aid

Other chapters of this book include information about some first aid procedures. The purpose of this chapter is to provide additional details about first aid procedures that can be invaluable when a serious submersion injury occurs. Many people who have taken CPR classes think that they know how to do rescue breathing and CPR, but there are more advanced techniques people can learn that can make the difference between life and death for submersion injury victims. This chapter will familiarize rescuers with additional first aid techniques for submersion victims to help them be better prepared for medical emergencies. Familiarization does not mean competency; equipment, training, techniques, and practice are required.

Learning Goals   By the end of this chapter, you should be able to:

▶ List several items of first aid equipment for aquatic emergencies that are not normally included in standard first aid kits.

▶ List the principal components of an oxygen delivery system and identify three types of oxygen delivery devices.

▶ State the recommended first aid training for basic, intermediate, and advanced providers.

▶ Describe the recommended procedure for removing wet clothing from a victim of an aquatic accident.

▶ Describe how to deliver heated oxygen to a submersion injury victim.

▶ Explain the value of cricoid pressure and describe the process.

▶ Describe basic airway suctioning techniques.

▶ Explain how to position victims who have various medical problems.

▶ Explain when and how to roll submersion injury victims.

▶ Explain the differences between controlling bleeding in a land-based accident and controlling bleeding in an aquatic emergency.

▶ Describe the first aid procedures for marine life injuries including stings, venomous puncture wounds, scrapes, and allergic reactions.

▶ Explain the primary benefit of practicing first aid skills and state when and how you should practice.

▶ List three recommended sources for medical emergency preparedness training.

Equipment

The more remote from medical care your aquatic activity is, the more prepared you should be in terms of equipment and preparedness. Figure 9.1 lists items to include in an aquatic first aid kit in addition to the equipment in a standard first aid kit.

Do not think that emergency oxygen equipment is only for professional rescuers. High-flow oxygen is of such value to submersion injury victims that anyone can take an oxygen first aid course and purchase emergency oxygen equipment. Prescriptions are needed for long-term, low-flow oxygen, but most states do not require them for high-flow, emergency use. By investing a few hours of your time and a few hundred dollars, you can qualify to administer oxygen. When you think of the value of saving lives, the cost of having oxygen at remote aquatic locations is quite small.

An oxygen delivery system consists of a cylinder, a pressure-reducing regulator, and several delivery devices (see figure 9.2). A good rule for cylinders is to have one or more to provide at least one hour of high-flow oxygen to an

- Appropriate medical emergency handbook (e.g., for scuba diving emergencies)
- Emergency action plan (see chapter 11)
- Rescue breathing mask
- Towels
- Blankets
- Trauma shears (for cutting clothing and exposure suits)
- Oxygen delivery system: cylinder, valve, regulator, and masks
- Manual suction system (to keep the airway clear)
- One gallon of drinking water
- One bottle of sterile eye irrigation solution
- One quart of vinegar (for venomous stings)
- Two elastic bandages (4" × 60")
- Large pressure bandages or pads (for severe bleeding)
- Six triangular bandages
- Deluxe, fine-tipped tweezers
- Forceps
- Sharp, scalpel-like knife
- Venom extraction kit (Sawyer "Extractor")
- Epinephrine kit (EpiPen)
- Inexpensive stethoscope (to listen to lung sounds)
- At least six chemical heat packs
- At least one hot water bottle
- Penlight or flashlight
- Pen and paper (for notes)
- Two-way radio or cell phone
- Backboard with straps

Figure 9.1 Recommended equipment.

injured person. Simple oxygen rebreather systems can increase the duration of an oxygen supply many times and should be considered when evacuations times can be lengthy.

Oxygen regulators may be constant flow, adjustable flow, demand, or a combination of adjustable flow and demand (see figure 9.3). The combination regulator, such as the one included in the oxygen system available from the Divers Alert Network, is desirable because the device can be used in a variety

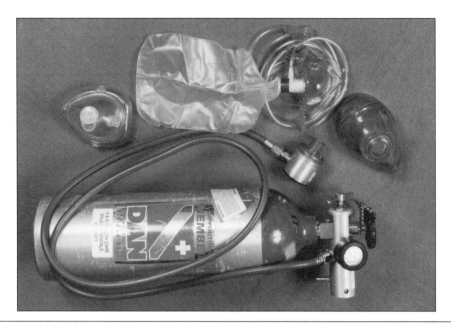

Figure 9.2 An oxygen delivery system consists of a cylinder, a regulator, and various delivery devices.

Figure 9.3 Oxygen regulator types include constant flow (upper left), adjustable flow (upper and lower right), and combination types (lower left).

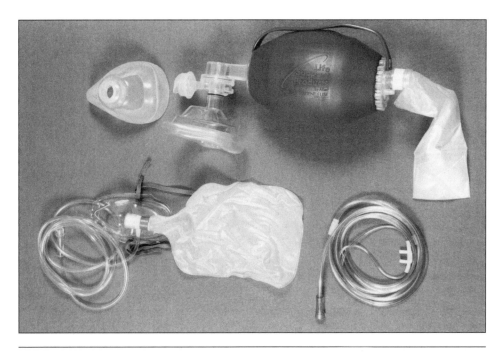

Figure 9.4 Common oxygen delivery devices include a Tru-fit mask (upper left), a bag-valve mask (BVM) (upper right), a non-rebreather mask (lower left), and a nasal cannula (lower right).

of situations. Constant or variable flow systems should be capable of providing at least 15 liters per minute.

Delivery devices include nasal cannulas, which are inappropriate for emergency oxygen administration, nonrebreather masks, and tight-fitting masks for demand valve breathing. A demand valve delivers oxygen on demand, for example, when the patient breathes. Demand valves allow rescuers to deliver 100 percent oxygen to breathing victims, such as scuba divers suffering from decompression illness. Nonrebreather masks also require victims to be breathing (see figure 9.4). When a victim is not breathing, the rescuer breathes from a mask and exhales the breathed oxygen into the victim.

Training

Equipment will not be of much value unless you know how to use it. The more medical training that you complete, the better the care you will be able to provide to a victim of submersion injuries. Table 9.1 lists different levels of medical training courses you might want to consider. I recommend at least the intermediate-level courses for anyone who is likely to render first aid in a remote aquatic location.

Organizations offering quality training sources for CPR and first aid include the American Heart Association, the National Safety Council, and the American

Table 9.1   Medical Training Courses

Basic	Intermediate	Advanced
Adult, child, and infant CPR	Healthcare provider CPR	First responder or emergency medical technician
Standard first aid	Advanced first aid	Advanced airway management
	Wilderness first aid	
	Oxygen first aid	

Red Cross. The Divers Alert Network offers several excellent oxygen first aid courses. Government agencies, such as fire departments and law enforcement agencies, often send members to first responder and EMT courses.

Training is valid for a limited time—usually two years. Repeat training is necessary to refresh skills and update knowledge. A surprising number of people truly believe that they know how to do CPR, but they have inadequate skills and incorrect knowledge. I recommend that you stagger your training and take one or two classes per year. A good schedule would be CPR and first aid one year and oxygen first aid the next year.

Techniques

First aid priorities for a submersion injury victim are the same as those for any unconscious person: airway, breathing, and circulation (ABC). The airway—the passage from the nose and mouth to the lungs—must be clear. Proponents of the Heimlich maneuver recommend its use for clearing the airways of submersion injury victims, but the American Heart Association Guidelines 2000 states that "Abdominal thrusts cause regurgitation of gastric contents and subsequent aspiration and have been associated with other injuries. Use the Heimlich maneuver only if the rescuer suspects foreign-body airway obstruction." I recommend visually inspecting the mouth and draining any visible water, but avoiding the Heimlich maneuver unless absolutely necessary to clear the airway.

All rescuers should have current CPR and first aid training. The CPR training should be at the healthcare provider level; basic CPR training can be inadequate in an aquatic emergency situation. CPR-trained rescuers should know how to establish an airway using the head-tilt, chin-lift method when there is no possibility of a spinal injury or with the jaw-thrust method if the possibility of a spinal cord injury exists.

With the airway clear and open, the rescuer assesses breathing by looking, listening, and feeling. Several possibilities exist. The victim may be breathing adequately. Breathing may be present, but inadequate. Breathing may be present, but with gurgling sounds. Or breathing may be absent. Breathing is considered adequate when the victim breathes at least every five seconds and when the chest visibly rises and falls. When breathing is inadequate or when the victim is in respiratory arrest, begin rescue breathing. When gurgling sounds are present, there is fluid in the airway; this must be drained to prevent further aspiration. Roll the victim to the right side, drain the airway, and then reposition the victim on the back.

Rescue breathing is not a simple task. Submersion injury victims seem to have an endless supply of water in their airways. Those who succumb in saltwater will have foam coming from their mouths and noses. Inflating the lungs will be more difficult than it would be for a victim without water in the lungs. You must keep clearing the airway. Ignore foam, but don't ignore gurgling. Roll and drain the victim as often as required. Even a makeshift suction device can be invaluable. A simple turkey baster is a handy item for aquatic first aid kits.

The recommendations in the paragraphs that follow are not intended for use in lieu of training, but as a supplement to your education. Instructors who teach CPR may not address in detail the procedures for victims of submersion injuries. First aid instructors will not teach you what to do for an injured scuba diver. And oxygen first aid instructors will not teach you the airway skills that are described in this section. My hope is that the combination of your training and the techniques in this chapter will help you successfully handle a submersion victim (see figure 9.5).

Figure 9.5 Well-managed first aid scenario.

THREE TRAINED LAY RESCUERS pull a clothed, unconscious victim from cold water at a lake on the outskirts of a city. One of the rescuers has already summoned emergency medical services. The possibility of a spinal cord injury has been eliminated. One rescuer assesses the victim's respiration and circulation while a second rescuer uses trauma shears to cut away the victim's wet clothing. The third rescuer, who has returned from phoning 911, prepares first aid equipment and notes the time.

The first rescuer finds that the victim is not breathing. The rescuer checks the mouth to ensure that the airway is clear and gives two slow breaths using a rescue breathing mask handed to him by the third rescuer. The second rescuer begins toweling the victim dry and covers him with a blanket. The first rescuer checks for a pulse while reassessing breathing and finds that the victim has a slow, weak heartbeat, but is still not breathing. The second rescuer takes an oxygen mask from the third rescuer and holds it near the face of the first rescuer, who inhales the oxygen and breathes it into the victim. The second rescuer uses his free hand to apply pressure to the proper location on the victim's neck to help prevent air from going into the victim's stomach and keep regurgitation from entering the airway. The third rescuer—knowing that submersion victims ingest large quantities of water and often regurgitate—has prepared a manual suction unit as a precautionary measure to keep the airway clear. The first rescuer reassesses the victim's breathing and circulation every minute.

As the sound of a siren increases, the third rescuer leaves the victim to flag the responding emergency unit and direct the medical personnel to the patient. The first rescuer gives a verbal report to the emergency medical personnel, and the third rescuer provides written notes. The EMS personnel transport the victim to a medical facility. The victim survives and recovers completely. The three rescuers are elated. The victim and his family are grateful. All of the training, equipment, and practice that prepared the rescuers for the few minutes of aid that they provided were worth every second and every penny because life is priceless.

The scenario presented in this section would be less than perfect if there were only one rescuer or if emergency medical services were not available. It would be less than perfect if the rescuers did not have emergency equipment or did not know how to use it. And the situation would be less than perfect without prompt evacuation to a medical facility. By breaking down each part of the scenario as follows, I will highlight the key techniques for submersion injury first aid.

One rescuer assesses the victim's respiration and circulation while a second rescuer uses trauma shears to cut away the victim's wet clothing. Hypothermia must be treated simultaneously with other immediate threats to life. Trauma shears are the best way to remove wet clothing rapidly (see figure 9.6). Tugging and pulling clothing can be rough and can cause the victim's heart to lose its rhythm. A wet victim continues to lose heat. Getting the victim dry is a priority to prevent

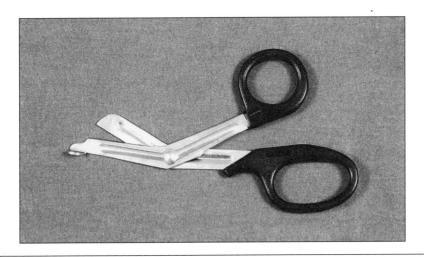

Figure 9.6 Trauma shears are an essential first aid tool.

additional heat loss.

The third rescuer, who has returned from phoning 911, prepares first aid equipment and notes the time. Emergency medical teams usually assign one person to manage the equipment. The person may also document events if no other personnel are available. The equipment person knows every skill that will be needed and the equipment that will be required. Anticipating each need, a good equipment person will have equipment ready for use when it is needed. A written history of times, actions, and victim responses is extremely valuable.

The second rescuer takes an oxygen mask from the third rescuer and holds it near the face of the first rescuer, who inhales the oxygen and breathes it into the victim. Submersion injury victims need the highest concentration of oxygen possible, but the oxygen must be warm and moist. Cold, dry oxygen as it comes from an oxygen cylinder is inappropriate because breathing cold gas causes more heat loss. Prebreathing oxygen warms the gas to body temperature and humidifies it. Humidified gas carries heat into the victim's lungs, which surround the heart. Because you use only 5 percent of the oxygen breathed, it is possible to deliver 95 percent oxygen to a victim when you prebreathe 100 percent oxygen. Even if you prebreathe only 50 percent oxygen, you will provide a victim with more than three times as much oxygen as he would receive from expired air rescue breathing.

The second rescuer uses his free hand to apply pressure to the proper location on the victim's neck to help prevent air from going into the victim's stomach and keep regurgitation from entering the airway. Pressure correctly applied to the cricoid cartilage in the neck, a skill developed in healthcare provider CPR classes, is invaluable for submersion victims. Regurgitated stomach contents are a frequent finding in the lungs of submersion victims during autopsy. Airway management and protection are extremely difficult in field situations. Cricoid pressure is a simple, effective technique to prevent fluid aspiration.

The third rescuer—knowing that submersion victims ingest large quantities of

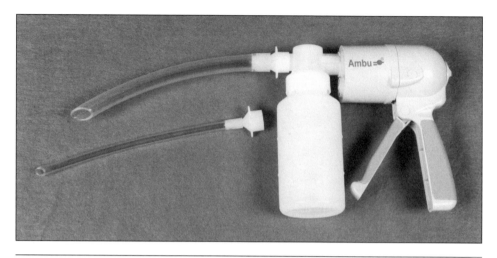

Figure 9.7 A simple, inexpensive manual suctioning device can be invaluable for an aquatic medical emergency.

water and often regurgitate—has prepared a manual suction unit as a precautionary measure to keep the airway clear. The better the airway management, the greater the victim's chances of survival. Cricoid pressure must be continuous until the victim is intubated. Even a momentary release of pressure will flood the airway. Monitor the sounds of breathing or rescue breathing. A gurgling sound means that immediate action must be taken to clear fluid from the airway. Manual suctioning is the best technique to remove the fluid. In the absence of suctioning equipment, you must log-roll the patient onto one side and drain the airway. Manual suctioning equipment, such as that shown in figure 9.7, is not prohibitively expensive, is highly reliable, and is easy to use. Insert the tip of the unit into the victim's mouth only as far as you can see. Suction an adult for no more than 15 seconds, a child for no more than 10 seconds, and an infant for no more than 5 seconds. Keep in mind that you are suctioning air from the victim's lungs in addition to fluid from the airway. Provide rescue breathing at a faster-than-normal rate for one or two minutes following suctioning.

Victim Positioning

The position in which you place a victim is an important part of first aid. Correct positioning helps save lives (see figure 9.8, *a-d*). The basic positions are as follows:

- Supine—flat on the back
- Standard shock—supine with feet and legs elevated
- Recovery—on the side
- Fowler's—on the back with the head and shoulders elevated
- Trendelenberg—on the back with the feet elevated

a

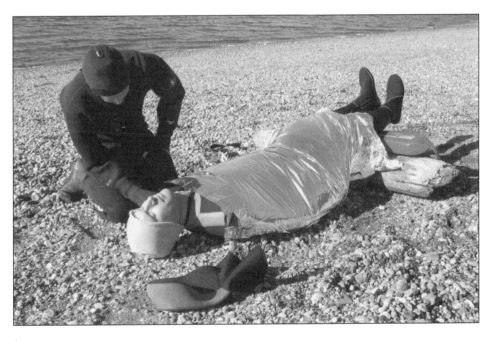

b

Figure 9.8 *(a)* Supine position, *(b)* standard shock position, *(c)* recovery position, and *(d)* Fowler's position. The Trendelenberg position should not be used.

c

d

Figure 9.8 *(continued)*

Submersion injury victims should be removed from the water in a horizontal position and kept horizontal until evaluated by a physician. Unconscious victims are placed in a supine position for assessment, rescue breathing, and CPR. Gurgling sounds heard during rescue breathing require the victim to be rolled to the side to clear the airway if suctioning is not available. Submersion injury victims will need to have their airways cleared frequently. When fluid is in the airway, a victim should be rolled to the *right* side. The right mainstem bronchi goes nearly straight into the right lung, whereas the left mainstem bronchi goes into the left lung at an angle. Fluid aspiration from a submersion injury goes into the right lung and disrupts normal function. Rolling a victim to the right side to clear fluid from an airway helps protect the left lung, which may be uninjured. Unconscious victims who have clear airways and are breathing spontaneously usually are placed on the *left* side because the stomach is on that side. Keeping the stomach low helps reduce regurgitation. A conscious, breathing victim may be placed on either side because muscle tone closes the esophagus and prevents regurgitation.

Victims who may have a spinal cord injury should be kept in a supine position. If you must roll the victim to clear the airway, use a log roll (see figure 9.9). Two

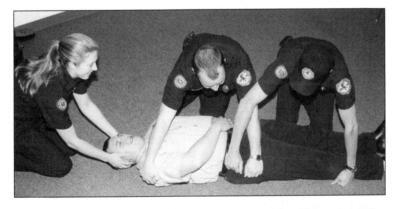

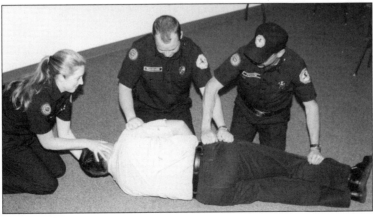

Figure 9.9 The log-roll technique for rolling a victim who may have a spinal cord injury. The head, neck, and spine are kept straight throughout the roll.

to four rescuers are needed for a log roll. One rescuer holds the head in a neutral position, and the other rescuers roll the body on a signal from the rescuer at the head. The head, neck, and spine are maintained in a straight line throughout the roll. As soon as the victim's airway is clear, the rescuers log-roll the victim back to a supine position on a signal from the rescuer at the head. If you are alone and must roll a victim who may have a spinal cord injury, place the victim's right arm up alongside the head and use it to support the victim's head while you roll the victim to the side. Place one hand behind the victim's head and steady it as much as possible while you roll the victim. Use your other hand to roll the victim's body.

The shock position has limited use for aquatic first aid, especially when the water is cold. Elevating the feet and legs of a hypothermic victim could cause heart rhythm disturbances and death. On the other hand, a victim who has lost a large amount of blood and who is pulled from warm water should be treated for shock. Think before you position a victim.

Victims who have head injuries or difficulty breathing qualify for the Fowler's position. Stabilize the head of any victim who has a head injury because a neck injury is likely.

For many years the Trendelenberg position was the standard first aid position for an injured scuba diver. Many experienced divers still believe this position is appropriate, but elevating the feet higher than the head should be avoided. The Trendelenberg position increases regurgitation and airway problems, causes the brain to swell, increases breathing difficulty, and has not been proven to be of any value. "Supine is fine" is a good, general rule for victims of submersion injuries unless they have fluid in the airway or are breathing, in which case they should be positioned on the side.

Horizontal means horizontal. CPR is not effective if a victim's head is elevated on a sloping beach or in a vessel that is underway with the bow higher than the stern. Place victims parallel to the water on a beach and athwartship on a boat.

Controlling Bleeding

Standard first aid recommends direct pressure, elevation, and pressure points to control bleeding and advises against the use of tourniquets. Some aquatic emergencies, such as boat propeller injuries and shark bites, may require more drastic measures to prevent death from blood loss. A nurse in Florida saved her boyfriend's life after a shark attack by using a piece of dental floss to tie off a severed artery deep inside a wound. Placing dressings over a severed artery that is spurting blood deep inside a wound may fail to stop the bleeding. Placing a gloved hand directly into the wound and applying pressure directly to the artery with the fingertips may be more effective. When a limb is bleeding severely from multiple deep propeller blade cuts, a tourniquet may be essential to prevent rapid, excessive blood loss. Severe bleeding must be controlled rapidly at remote locations or a victim will die from shock.

Marine Life Injuries

Entire books have been written on this subject, and people who are likely to sustain injuries from marine animals should have reference books available. The purpose of this brief section is to increase your awareness of specialized first aid procedures for marine life injuries.

Swimmers and scuba divers who are not prepared, observant, and careful may be bitten, stung, stuck, or scraped. Venomous wounds may cause life-threatening conditions. Some injuries, such as stings from certain jellyfish, can incapacitate a victim in the water and pose a threat to rescuers handling a victim. Familiarity with hazardous marine animals and how to deal with injuries from them is an important part of preparation for an aquatic activity.

Most injuries occur from lack of protection, wading, or handling or provoking animals. Swimmers and divers should wear exposure suits, shuffle their feet when moving in shallow water, avoid contact with animals, and avoid provocation. People who do not heed sound advice and ignore safe practices will need first aid.

Jellyfish, fire coral, some sponges, and plantlike animals called hydroids can inflict painful stings. Coral, sponge, and hydroid stings and most jellyfish stings are painful, but several types of jellyfish stings can be life threatening. When a jellyfish stings a victim, immediately assist the person from the water and use seawater and tweezers to flush and remove any residual material from the skin. Apply vinegar-soaked compresses until the pain is relieved. Monitor the victim continuously and treat for shock. Seek medical care. For less severe stings, follow the same procedures, but coat the injury with hydrocortisone lotion in lieu of medical care.

Cone shells, spiny fish, stingrays, sea snakes, some starfish, and sea urchins inflict venomous puncture wounds, some of which are life threatening and require antivenin. Know the animals in the area and where to seek medical care in the event of a serious marine life injury. There are two basic first aid procedures. Extremely venomous injuries require different techniques than those that are less venomous. Puncture wounds from fish, stingrays, sea urchins, and the crown-of-thorns starfish should be treated by removing any visible material from the wound and soaking the injured area in hot, nonscalding (110 degrees Fahrenheit) water for one to one and one-half hours. Allow the wound to remain open and seek medical care.

First aid procedures differ for extremely venomous wounds such as those of cone shells, sea snakes, or the Australian blue-ringed octopus. Use the pressure-immobilization technique for a wound to a limb (see figure 9.10). Place a pad over the wound and wrap a splint to the limb from top to bottom with an elastic bandage. The bandage should be snug, but should not prevent circulation to the extremities. Fingers and toes should remain pink and have normal sensation. Treat the victim for shock and monitor continuously. Take the victim directly to a medical facility. Except for sea snake bites, which are extremely rare, avoid the temptation to attempt incisions and apply suction.

Figure 9.10   The pressure-immobilization technique is useful for venomous aquatic injuries.

Scrapes from coral and barnacles can become infected. First aid consists primarily of cleaning the wound thoroughly and applying an antibacterial ointment. Scrub the wound vigorously with soap, water, and a brush and rinse the wound thoroughly with running water or with water under pressure from a syringe. Apply ointment and a loose, dry, sterile dressing. Repeat the treatment twice daily. Seek medical care if the wound indicates signs of infection.

Injuries from marine animals may cause some victims to experience an adverse allergic reaction. Anaphylactic shock from an allergic reaction can rapidly become life threatening. Indications include shock; breathing difficulty; swelling of the lips, tongue, and throat; itchy, blotchy skin; and possibly seizures. An immediate injection with epinephrine is essential. People with known severe allergies who travel to remote areas should carry epinephrine auto-injectors, such as the Epi-Pen, and should instruct those accompanying them on how to use the device (see figure 9.11).

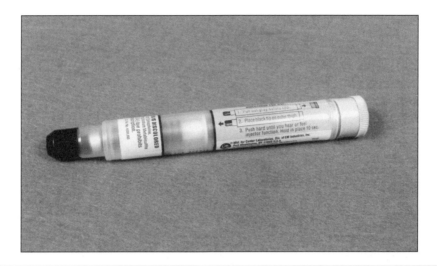

Figure 9.11   An epinephrine auto-injector can save the life of a person experiencing an allergic reaction. The effect of the medication is temporary, so more than one injector may be required for remote locations.

When you engage in aquatic activities, your first aid kit needs to include supplies for injuries that may be sustained from local aquatic animals. Be sure that your supplies include tweezers, elastic bandages, splints, and—for saltwater areas—vinegar.

Practice

Equipment and skills are not useful unless you practice. People tend to believe that once they have learned a skill, they will retain it indefinitely, but skill performance clearly deteriorates as time passes. Professionals know that skills must be repeated until the actions become automatic—without concentrated effort—and then those skills must be practiced often to retain proficiency.

One of the greatest benefits of skill proficiency is psychological. Your ability to analyze a situation while at the same time thinking about how to perform physically is severely hampered in an emergency because of chemical changes in your body caused by the excitement of the moment. Skills that can be executed correctly without concentrated effort allow you to concentrate your efforts on analyzing the situation. Rescuers who are competent, cool, and calm in an emergency are clearly thinking about the situation much more than about what they are doing to care for the victim. You can realize the same benefit by practicing rescue and first aid skills (see figure 9.12).

Whenever you practice water rescue and first aid skills, be sure to inform bystanders, lifeguards, and anyone who may misinterpret the situation and become concerned. It is embarrassing and inappropriate to have police, fire, and EMS personnel arrive when there is no actual emergency. I always ask those

Figure 9.12 Practice first aid skills periodically so you will be able to recall them when they are actually needed.

posing as victims to hold up one hand and form an OK sign with their thumb and forefinger. I also establish two signals: one for a true emergency that might occur during a practice session, and one for a person acting the role of a victim to signal a rescuer to stop the scenario.

Vary your practice methods. One practice method is to focus on a specific skill. Tell everyone what the skill is in advance, discuss the procedures, perform the skill, and then discuss the proceedings. Another practice method is to create a scenario that requires multiple skills. Describe the situation, but do not discuss the techniques in advance. Correct errors as they occur instead of waiting until afterward and telling participants what they did wrong. Repeat the same scenario until the participants can perform the skills correctly without being coached. At the highest level of practice, participants receive no feedback from the evaluator until after skill completion. This evaluation method is appropriate for professional rescuers, but is likely to frustrate lay rescuers. Keep in mind that the purpose of practice is to increase the confidence of rescuers, not to cause them to feel inadequate.

When and where you practice is just as important as how you practice. If you practice only in ideal weather and water conditions, you are not being realistic. Learn skills in ideal conditions, but practice them in reasonable, realistic circumstances. Practicing in severe conditions is foolish unless you are a professional, trained and qualified to respond when the weather and water conditions are poor. The more realistic your practice sessions are, however, the better you will be at coping with an actual emergency. Consider the fact that accidents often occur when people are fatigued at the end of a day of water activity. Learn skills when you are fresh, well rested, and full of energy, but practice them at the end of the day so you will know how to use them even when you are tired.

Devoting a few minutes to effective practice during every aquatic outing is better than devoting an entire day to the task. When a swimmer returns to a boat, use the opportunity to practice extrication. When a water skier falls, use that opportunity to deploy a rescue swimmer for a practice rescue. Practice does not need to be a big production.

Perhaps the best time to practice rescue and first aid procedures is at the beginning of the aquatic season. Review the emergency action plan (see chapter 11) with the participants. Review the skill steps. Practice the physical skills and discuss the procedures. Get everyone involved to understand how to respond. A small amount of preparation and practice for water emergencies can be just as invaluable as discussing and practicing a fire drill at home.

Combine the practice of rescue and first aid skills. People tend to stop a drill when they extricate a victim from the water because they are exhausted from the rescue. Once the victim is out of the water, other rescuers can then take over and practice providing first aid. Practice cutting old clothing from a wet victim, drying the person, and helping to maintain body heat. Practice positioning and rolling victims. Practice the deployment of first aid equipment. Practice every skill that you may need to save a person's life.

The frequency of practice varies. Professional rescuers practice at least quarterly. Lay rescuers should rehearse water rescue and first aid skills at least twice a year. If you live in a warm climate, practice skills every six months. If you live in a cold climate, practice skills twice during the season in which you participate in aquatic activities.

Sources

You must be wondering where—short of becoming an emergency medical technician—you could possibly obtain the skills and equipment described in this chapter. Emergency medicine is not as complicated and complex as it once was. More training and equipment is available to the lay rescuer than ever before.

I recommend the American Heart Association or the National Safety Council CPR and first aid courses, and the Divers Alert Network oxygen first aid courses. Contact information for these organizations is included in appendix A. Also consider seeking out opportunities to complete either a first responder or emergency medical technician course.

Oxygen delivery systems and first aid kits are available from the Divers Alert Network. Additional supplies are available at drugstores and from medical supply companies. Your doctor can supply prescriptions for emergency medications, such as epinephrine. The important point to remember is that if you truly want to be prepared for an emergency, you can obtain everything that you need.

Key Points

Equipment, training, and practicing needed skills using the equipment are essential for emergency preparedness. Obtain and keep current CPR, first aid, and oxygen first aid training. Obtain and inventory frequently first aid equipment and an oxygen delivery system. Practice the techniques of resuscitation, positioning, and other first aid procedures that may be needed. As you participate in training, you will discover many sources for equipment and for higher levels of training. Take advantage of every opportunity to learn more about emergency medicine. The day will come when you and the person whose life you save will be extremely grateful that you made the effort to acquire the needed knowledge, skills, and equipment.

Chapter 10

Evacuations

Professional rescuers normally coordinate evacuations, but you may find yourself in a situation in which emergency personnel are unable to respond. You may have to assist with the evacuation of a victim to a medical facility. The evacuation may take place by water, air, or ground transportation. Factors affecting evacuation means include injury severity, time and distance to the nearest medical facility, accident location, weather conditions, and number of victims.

Air ambulances typically do not take patients who require CPR, and they will not respond when fog limits visibility. When an accident scene is remote, rugged, and steep, high-angle rope rescue teams may be needed to take the patient to a more favorable location for evacuation. Strong winds and rough water conditions may prevent an evacuation that could be accomplished with more favorable conditions. You must consider all options and be flexible; familiarization with a few simple procedures can help you avoid problems that can occur during evacuations.

MY WIFE AND I WERE SCUBA DIVING from a charter boat in a remote location when one of the divers lost consciousness and aspirated water. I rescued the young man and was able to get him breathing again, but he remained unconscious. The charter boat was slow. It had taken us over two hours to reach our diving destination, and the victim could not wait two hours for treatment. The captain of our vessel radioed boats in the area and was able to obtain the assistance of a speedboat. The captain also was able to get an ambulance enroute to meet us at a resort that was about halfway back to the city. We transferred the victim to the speedboat and took him rapidly to the resort. When we reached the resort, the ambulance had not arrived, so we loaded the victim into a taxi and drove toward the city until we encountered the ambulance. We stopped the ambulance and transferred the victim to the emergency medical personnel. We followed the ambulance to the medical facility and reported what had happened to the emergency room physicians. We also had the doctors phone the Divers Alert Network to obtain specialized information on how to assess and treat scuba diving injuries. The young man recovered completely partly because we were able to analyze our resources and be flexible to achieve the goals of a safe and rapid evacuation.

Learning Goals *By the end of this chapter, you should be able to:*

- ▶ List five factors affecting the evacuation of a submersion injury victim.
- ▶ State the two primary objectives of an evacuation and list two additional objectives.
- ▶ Explain how to position a victim for evacuation in a boat.
- ▶ Describe several methods of keeping a victim warm during evacuation.
- ▶ Explain how to monitor a victim's condition during evacuation.
- ▶ Describe three types of water airlift evacuations.
- ▶ Describe the general procedures for a ground airlift evacuation.
- ▶ Describe the general procedures for ground transportation evacuation.

Evacuation Objectives

When a victim is in critical condition, the most important objective when determining evacuation is safety for everyone involved. The second critical objective is time. The faster the victim receives medical treatment, the better the chances of a full recovery will be.

In addition to the objectives of safe and rapid transport, you also want to keep submersion victims horizontal, maintain high-flow oxygen administration, avoid rough handling, prevent heat loss, and monitor the victim's status constantly. The physical factors affecting evacuations can make the achievement of your goals challenging.

Another important evacuation objective is to send information with the victim. Send identification, medical history, accident history, a record of first aid actions, and any changes in the victim's condition. Actions and changes should have times recorded.

Whenever possible, send someone with the victim to the medical facility or have someone go to the medical facility as quickly as safely possible. Evacuating the uninjured buddy of a scuba diver is a common practice because the diver who is apparently all right may develop symptoms later and require treatment. If ambulance personnel are reluctant to allow you to ride in the ambulance with the victim, tell them that you have information that will be needed at the medical facility and ask if you can ride in the front seat of the ambulance or aid unit.

Water Transport Evacuations

Evacuation by boat usually is not a good option unless the victim's injuries are not serious and the person's condition is stable. Boats are slow and they bounce. In small, open boats, the victim is exposed to the elements. When a victim is in critical condition and aboard a vessel, consider other options. Arrange an airlift or take the victim to the nearest place on shore where ground transportation can be arranged.

When you must transport by watercraft, keep the evacuation objectives in mind and strive to meet them. Positioning a victim in a small boat is tricky because the angle of the boat may be unfavorable to the victim when the boat rises to a cruising position. If you must place the victim with the head toward the bow or the stern of a small boat, it is best to have the person on a backboard so you can place objects beneath one end of the board to keep it level. When the water is rough and the boat rolls from side to side, placing the victim in line with the long axis of the vessel is better than a position across the vessel. Use your best judgment initially to avoid moving the victim any more than necessary. If the position becomes unfavorable, however, reposition the victim to keep him as level as possible.

Because water transports are slow and because the best first aid for submersion injury victims is high-concentration oxygen, consider obtaining an oxygen rebreather system (see figure 10.1). When you take an oxygen first aid course, you can complete an additional module that will qualify you to use the rebreather, which can extend the length of time for a standard oxygen bottle up to six hours. An advantage of the chemical process of a rebreather is that the gas is warmed and humidified—two essential features of oxygen administration for a submersion victim.

Hypothermic victims must be handled as gently as possible (see chapter 3). Rough handling can cause the heart to lose its normal rhythm. Moving the boat more slowly and taking longer to reach your destination may be better than bouncing and jostling the victim by going faster. This is one of the many compromise situations in first aid. Think to place padding beneath the victim when you position her initially. The less you move a cold victim, the better.

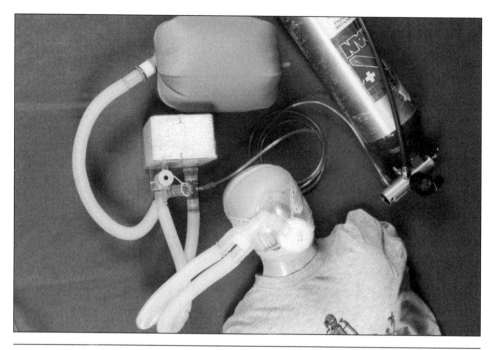

Figure 10.1   An oxygen rebreather system can make a cylinder of oxygen last hours versus minutes and is recommended for aquatic activities in remote locations.

Preventing heat loss can be difficult in a small boat when conditions are poor. The victim must be dry and insulated. Mylar foil blankets help retain radiant heat and reduce wind chill better than cloth blankets. Plastic-backed foam emergency blankets are excellent when placed over Mylar blankets. Remember to dry and cover the victim's head. Mylar caps or knitted wool caps are excellent options. Use external heat packs only when the victim is profoundly hypothermic and transport will be more than an hour. Remember to wrap heat packs in cloth because placing them directly on the skin of a hypothermic victim can cause burns. Because of impaired circulation, the victim is unable to distribute the heat in a normal manner.

Monitoring an unconscious victim in a moving vessel is another difficult task. Check airway, breathing, circulation, mental status, and neurological status every few minutes. If the victim is breathing oxygen, humidity that forms in the mask with each breath is a good way to determine breathing status. The presence of a pulse in the victim's wrist is a good way to assess circulation in a conscious victim. Use the artery in the neck if the victim in unconscious. Assess neurological status in conscious victims by having them raise their eyebrows, stick out their tongues, follow your finger with their eyes, and wiggle their fingers and toes. Ask if they are experiencing any abnormal sensations such as tingling, burning, or numbness.

Airlift Transport Evacuations

In remote or rugged areas you may need to airlift a victim to a medical facility. The evacuation may occur on water or from land. This section covers some basic safety procedures that you need to know if you are called on to assist with an air evacuation.

Water Airlifts

The choice of airlift technique will depend on the situation, the distance to shore, the aircraft, and the crew members. Helicopter rescue teams may rescue victims from the water and lift them aboard the aircraft. A long-line rescue is a method that may be used near shore (see figure 10.2). A rescuer deployed from the helicopter places a victim into a sling and the helicopter carries both people to the shore and gently lowers them to the ground.

Figure 10.2 A long-line evacuation.

Victims also may be evacuated from a boat that is stationary or moving. Air ambulances—helicopters with special medical equipment and personnel—do not accept patients who require CPR since the interruption of resuscitation during transfer would be excessive. Use alternate evacuation methods when a victim is in cardiac arrest.

When you are notified that a helicopter is being dispatched to your location for an evacuation from a boat, you must prepare your vessel. Anything that could be blown away by a 150-mph wind must be stowed or secured. Loss is not the primary concern. When a helicopter hovers, a strong downdraft blows loose objects laterally. The air then rises upward where it is pulled into the helicopter engine's air intakes. As the helicopter nears, you should lower tall antennas.

For airlift evacuations from a boat, the helicopter will lower a line that will be charged with static electricity. Allow the line to touch the water or the boat before you touch it or you could be jolted. Never tie the line to the boat! Some air ambulances lower a crew member to a boat and then send down a litter basket for the patient. Smaller aircraft may only send down the litter basket. If a litter basket is lowered to your boat, disconnect the basket until the victim is completely packaged and ready to be lifted (see figure 10.3).

Figure 10.3 Airlift configuration for evacuation from a moving boat.

Figure 10.4 Airlift configuration for a moving airlift.

A victim being evacuated by air over water must wear a life jacket and must be well secured in the litter basket. Do not attempt to ride the litter with the victim. Do send identification and documentation with the victim.

Most helicopter pilots prefer to evacuate victims from boats that are moving instead of stationary (see figure 10.4). If the pilot instructs you to be underway for the evacuation, steer the vessel to keep the wind just to the side of the bow. The wind direction allows the pilot to maintain the helicopter in a position that affords an optimal view of the evacuation area. Maintain a constant speed throughout the operation. Direct radio communication with the pilot is highly desirable. Attempt to establish communication with the pilot before the helicopter arrives.

Ground Airlifts

Professional rescuers usually coordinate helicopter evacuations, which involve the establishment of a landing zone. A fire engine and emergency medical personnel are dispatched, whose flashing red lights help the pilot locate the landing area. A landing zone commander has constant radio communication with the pilot.

If instructed to select a landing zone for an air evacuation, seek an area 100 feet wide by 100 feet long that is flat and clear of obstructions and overhead wires (see figure 10.5). A parking lot or field is a good choice. Clear the landing zone of debris and unsecured items. If possible, establish radio communication with the helicopter and describe the landing zone, report the landing zone visibility and the wind direction and strength, and recommend the clearest approach direction. Avoid using white lights and white strobe lights at the landing zone

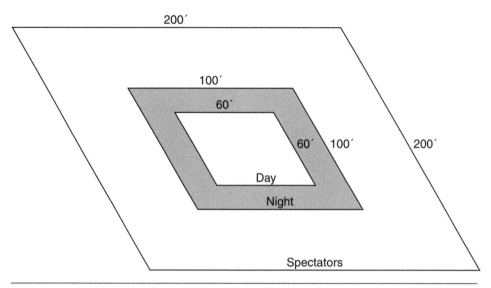

Figure 10.5 A landing zone for an air evacuation must be of adequate size, be clear of overhead obstructions, and have a slope not in excess of 10 degrees. Large helicopters require larger landing zones (up to 120 feet).

to protect the pilot's night vision. The use of red lights or flares is acceptable if the flares do not pose a fire hazard.

If possible, maintain communication with the pilot during the landing. Immediately notify the pilot of any safety issues. When the helicopter lands, remain clear until the rotor blades have stopped. Approach the aircraft only when directed by the flight crew and then only from the front. Follow all instructions from the flight crew. Clear everyone away from the helicopter before the pilot starts the engine for takeoff. Remain well clear of the aircraft and notify the pilot if any unsafe situation develops.

When an injured scuba diver must be evacuated by air, request the pilot to fly at the lowest possible altitude to avoid making the victim's condition worse by the lower pressures that result from high altitudes.

Ground Transport Evacuations

A TRAGEDY OCCURRED YEARS AGO when a scuba diving accident happened on a remote island in the Caribbean. Diving companions with good intentions were driving a victim to a medical facility for treatment. Reckless driving caused an accident that killed one person and severely injured another. The original victim, whose submersion injury was not severe, survived the motor vehicle crash and recovered completely.

In some remote areas the only means of evacuation may be by a motor vehicle. Remember that your vehicle is not an ambulance with red lights and a siren. Safe driving is the top priority; getting the victim to the medical facility is the second priority. I know from years of experience driving aid units and ambulances that speeding as opposed to driving the speed limit saves only a small amount of time. Unless a victim is being resuscitated, a couple of minutes will not affect the person's condition adversely.

Among the most difficult tasks related to transporting a patient by private vehicle are loading and positioning the victim. Remember to be as gentle as possible; keep the victim horizontal; and place a stable, breathing victim on the left side. Avoid twist lifting, which can cause a back injury. Plan how to load the victim and practice first using a person who is not injured.

Another difficult transport task is victim monitoring. Whenever possible, assign one rescuer to this task. The rescuer should be in a position to assess breathing, circulation, and mental status. The rescuer needs to be able to communicate with the driver. The vehicle may need to be stopped if the victim's status changes abruptly. The driver needs to keep in mind that the rescuer monitoring the victim is not restrained and could be injured from sudden turns and stops.

Key Points

Arrange professional evacuation whenever possible. When professional assistance is not feasible, consider the options and the factors affecting evacuation. Determine the safest and fastest method to get the victim to a medical facility. Also consider the evacuation objectives: Keep the victim horizontal, maintain high-flow oxygen administration, avoid rough handling, prevent heat loss, and monitor the victim's status constantly. Comply with instructions from emergency medical personnel. Do your best to establish and maintain communication with responding units, especially helicopters. Be sure to send important information with the victim. Above all, avoid harming the victim and any rescuers during an evacuation.

Chapter **11**

Emergency Action Plans

When a submersion injury happens, you will need more than training and equipment. You will also need the support of emergency medical personnel, evacuation services, and medical facilities. A well-thought-out emergency action plan specifically for your location will help you coordinate these important services. The more remote your activity, the more essential an emergency action plan becomes. This chapter covers the types of plans, their content, and their use.

Learning Goals *By the end of this chapter, you should be able to:*

- State the purposes of a hazard analysis survey, a resource analysis plan, a float plan, and an emergency action plan.
- List information resources for various emergency plans.
- Explain how to organize, use, store, and maintain emergency plans.

Hazard Analysis Survey

A hazard analysis survey is a valuable plan used by many agencies. By determining all possible hazards in advance of an activity, potential accidents may be anticipated and hopefully avoided. Appendix C contains a sample hazard analysis survey. Figure 11.1 lists typical hazards in aquatic environments. Use the survey form in appendix C to analyze each situation.

When planning an excursion to an unfamiliar area, contact people in advance and determine potential hazards (see figure 11.2). Information sources include charts, books, scuba stores, yacht clubs, and marine stores. Internet searches also are helpful.

- Water access (easy or difficult, distance to ground transportation and landing zone)
- Exit (shore, dock, boat)
- Depths (average, minimum, maximum, tide levels)
- Water temperature (at surface and at depth)
- Water clarity
- Bottom type (rock, sediment, debris)
- Entanglement (submerged trees, fishing line, nets)
- Entrapment (sucking holes, sucking currents, structures)
- Water movement (currents, waves, surf)
- Boat traffic (amount, type)
- Hazardous aquatic animals
- Pollution
- Weather conditions

Figure 11.1 Potential aquatic hazards.

Figure 11.2 Water hazards may include entanglement, waves, surf, and currents. Always know what to expect.

Resource Analysis Plan

A resource analysis is another valuable plan. This lists all of the resources available in the vicinity of your aquatic activity. The fewer the resources or the longer it takes them to reach your location (or you to reach theirs), the more preparation is required on your part. The following list contains typical resources that you might need to consider. Scuba divers need more resources than do swimmers, so you may not need to seek contact information for all of the resources listed.

Resource contact information:

- Emergency medical services (local seven-digit number for cell phone calls)
- Nearest medical facility (name, address, and phone number)
- Nearest physician (qualified to manage submersion or scuba injuries)
- Recompression chamber (where an injured scuba diver may be transferred)

- Nearest local marine search and rescue unit
- Local law enforcement unit
- Nearest airlift evacuation unit
- Emergency contact information for all participants (contact person name and phone number)

Obtaining this information in advance is not difficult, and it will save precious minutes during a life-threatening emergency. If you wait until a person's life is hanging in the balance and phone 911 on a cell phone, the delay that you experience until your call can be connected to a local EMS unit could be fatal. You need to be able to contact the needed personnel directly and immediately. Unless you are in or proximate to a city and have access to a standard telephone, you need to do a resource analysis to be properly prepared for an aquatic accident.

Float Plan

Another simple and valuable plan is a float plan for watercraft operators. The plan contains your destination, your vessel description and identification number, the course that you will follow, and your expected time of return. Figure 11.3 is an example of a float plan form. Anytime you operate a vessel, leave this plan with someone. Instruct the person to contact authorities and have them search for you if you have not checked in by a specified time.

Emergency Action Plan

The emergency action plan (EAP) is your final and most important plan. You use your hazard analysis survey and resource analysis plan to prepare an EAP that you will implement in the event of an accident. There are two types of EAPs: one for the local area that you prepare and update annually and the other for new areas. The latter must be developed in advance of each excursion. The information in table 11.1 should be included in your EAP.

Individual information is valuable in an emergency. Part of your EAP should include having each person participating in the excursion complete a participant emergency information card such as the one depicted in figure 11.4.

As you develop EAPs, you will find that some plans require more equipment and more self-reliance than other plans. When you prepare your plan, prepare a checklist of the emergency equipment you will need (see lists in previous chapters). Checklists help prevent omissions. I recommend one additional item for your EAP—a checklist of actions that you can consult in an emergency. Appendix D offers an example of an emergency action checklist. The list can help you remember the steps to take if you are unable to think clearly under stress.

Destination

Departure date and time _____

Planned return date and time _____

Location (general area) _____

Location (latitude and longitude) _____

Vessel Description

Make _____

Model _____

Vessel ID No. _____

Color _____

General description _____

Communications

Radio frequencies monitored _____

Cell phone number _____

Requested Action

If no contact by (date and time) _____,
contact authorities and request search and rescue.

Requested by _____

Date _____

Signature _____

Figure 11.3   Vessel float plan. Use this form to tell someone who is not going with you where you are going, how to reach you, and what to do if you do not return by a designated time.

From *Aquatic Rescue and Safety* by Dennis K. Graver, 2004, Champaign, IL: Human Kinetics.

Table 11.1   Emergency Action Plan

Component	Necessary information	Excursion details
Hazard analysis survey	Potential hazards	
	Plan to minimize risks posed by potential hazards	
Participants	Names	
	Medical conditions, history	
	Treatment authorization	
Resource analysis plan	Emergency contact names and phone numbers	
	Emergency resources contact information (phone numbers, radio frequencies, or both)	

From *Aquatic Rescue and Safety* by Dennis K. Graver, 2004, Champaign, IL: Human Kinetics.

In an emergency, please contact _____

Relationship _____ Phone (___)_____

Personal physician _____ Phone (___)_____

Medical conditions _____

Required medications _____

Allergies _____

Blood type _____ Date of birth_____

In an emergency, I hereby authorize medical treartment and/or treatment in a recompression chamber.

Signature _____ Date _____

Signature of parent or guardian if a minor _____

Figure 11.4 Emergency information card.

EAP Organization, Use, Storage, and Maintenance

Many people are reluctant to develop an EAP. Those who do develop a plan rarely update it for changing circumstances. If you consider the potential legal and moral consequences of not having and maintaining a plan, your attitude is likely to change. When you assume responsibility for the safety and well-being of others, an EAP can drastically reduce your liability. When you are properly prepared for an emergency and do all that you are trained to do, you have legal protection under the Good Samaritan law in nearly all states. When you have done all that you can to save a loved one, you will not feel guilty if the person does not survive an accident. Investing a little time and effort to develop an EAP can save a great deal of time and stress that may occur following a tragedy.

Your EAP should have several physical components (see figure 11.5). Avoid putting the entire plan on a single page. Emergency contact information cards—for resources and for participants—should be separate from your plan and stored in zippered plastic bags. The emergency action checklist also should be separate. When an emergency occurs, prepare the EAP package for use. Give the emergency resource information card to one person assigned to summon aid. Use the checklist to make sure that you include all of the important steps. Give the participant contact information card to emergency personnel.

Store your EAP where you can access it quickly in an emergency. A typical location is inside a first aid kit. Sealing the plan inside a vinyl page holder or laminating it is helpful because paper can become soaked quickly during an aquatic emergency. I recommend developing your plan with a computer and saving the file so you can update the plan and print out a new one at any time.

At the beginning of an aquatic activity, review the EAP with the participants (see figure 11.6). Make sure that the emergency contact information is current.

Hazard analysis survey

❑ Emergency equipment checklist
❑ Emergency action plan
❑ Emergency resources contact information
❑ Emergency information cards

Figure 11.5 Emergency action plan components.

Figure 11.6 Review your emergency action plan before you need to implement it.

Discuss potential hazards and how to avoid injuries. Familiarize participants with the location of the emergency equipment and discuss its use. Review how to summon assistance. Review and discuss the action checklist. All of these steps can be done while traveling and can help pass the time when you are going to your destination.

Key Points

Remember the five Ps: Proper Planning Prevents Poor Performance. If you want to perform well in an emergency, you need to plan for contingencies. After you determine where you want to go for your aquatic adventure, do some investigation to determine potential hazards. Find out how to contact emergency services in the area. Develop an EAP that minimizes the risk of injury and establishes the equipment that you will need. Prepare emergency contact information cards for emergency services and for the participants in your group. Prepare a checklist of emergency action steps. Protect your plan, checklist, and contact cards against water damage. Store the EAP package where it will be readily accessible. Review and revise the EAP information at least annually and prepare a new EAP whenever you go to a new area. Finally, remember to file a float plan every time your adventure involves the use of a watercraft.

Chapter 12

Legal Concerns

In today's society, most people are concerned about the possible legal implications of their actions. Injured and disabled victims often sue, and families of deceased victims may bring suit for wrongful death. Thankfully, citizens are provided some legal protection when rescuing submersion victims and providing first aid. Professionals are held to a higher standard called the standard of practice. Professional rescuers are required to do what other professionals with equivalent training and responsibility would do. The following information may help you avoid legal consequences if you choose to provide aid to the victim of a submersion accident. Laws vary from state to state. You should consult an attorney for precise information pertaining to your area.

- ▶ Define standard of practice, implied consent, expressed consent, and abandonment.
- ▶ Explain the Good Samaritan law.
- ▶ Explain your responsibility to assist in an emergency situation.
- ▶ Explain the slogan, Do no harm.
- ▶ List five of seven ways to help preserve evidence at a potential crime scene.
- ▶ Explain how to communicate with the media following an emergency situation.
- ▶ Explain the importance of training for both amateur and professional rescuers.

Citizens on shore are not required to render assistance to a person in distress in the water. Boaters are required to lend assistance to another vessel in distress. If citizens choose to provide help, most states offer protection from civil damages under Good Samaritan statutes (Limmer et al. 2001). The Good Samaritan law requires only that people providing aid act in good faith and do what they have training to do, nothing more.

The Good Samaritan law does not apply in three potential areas of liability. The first involves *consent for assistance*. Consent is implied when a victim is unconscious or incoherent, but conscious victims have the right to refuse assistance. If you force care on a person who refuses your help, you could be charged with assault and battery. An example is a person who has lost consciousness while immersed, has regained consciousness, and does not want further assistance. Use your powers of persuasion to convince the victim that she needs a medical evaluation and could die without medical care. Expressed consent is obtained when a competent adult victim gives permission for you to provide help. The affirmation may be only a nod of the head. Permission is not needed if the victim is a minor and parents are not present. If an adult victim remains uncooperative, wait for emergency medical personnel to arrive. You do not need a victim's permission to summon emergency medical services.

The second legal concern stems from injury to a victim caused by *moving the victim unnecessarily*. An example would be removing a victim with a neck injury from warm water when professional aid was nearby. If the victim suffered any neurological deficit, you could be held liable. Move victims only when absolutely necessary—do no harm. The victim should be no worse after you provide aid than he was before. Be especially wary about accidents in which a back or neck injury is likely.

The third potential legal problem occurs *if you begin providing first aid to a victim and then abandon your efforts before you are relieved by someone with qualifications equal to or greater than yours.* This principle does not apply to a rescue. If you try to rescue someone and realize that the situation is too great a risk, you may abandon a rescue without consequence. Do not abandon first aid procedures, however.

Professionals who respond to emergency calls for assistance have a greater responsibility to provide aid and are expected to do rescues and give aid at a higher level of care than citizens, abiding by the standard of care. Professionals— law enforcement officers, firefighters, emergency medical technicians, and paramedics—are people who are compensated for their services, no matter how small the compensation.

Professionals are more likely than citizens to be concerned with the preservation of evidence at the scene of an aquatic accident (see figure 12.1). Citizens should keep the following ideas in mind, however, because actions taken immediately following an incident can help resolve a serious legal dispute that may ensue. Actions that can help preserve evidence include the following:

- Safeguarding the area
- Noting any watercraft in the area and recording their registration numbers
- Safeguarding any tangible evidence
- Requesting witnesses to wait for the arrival of law enforcement personnel
- Taking photos of the area and water conditions
- Recording the wind and weather conditions and direction
- Taking detailed notes

Figure 12.1 Documentation is an important aspect of emergency procedures. If it happened, write it down; if you don't record it, it didn't happen!

Always try to write down what happens during and immediately after an accident. If possible, assign a person to record what you ask her to write. Record the facts, but not opinions. Actions and the times when the actions were taken are valuable facts. Names and addresses of people involved are valuable. Any complaints from a victim, objective information about the victim's condition, the victim's identity and medical history, and a brief explanation about what happened—all of these can be valuable.

Documentation is essential for professional rescuers, who know that if you didn't record something, legally it did not occur. The three most important rules for liability protection are document, document, and document. Paperwork done faithfully for small events prepares you for the important paperwork required for significant events. Develop a documentation procedure and use it for every water rescue response.

Media Communications

When an accident occurs, media response is common because news agencies scan emergency radio frequencies. Saying "no comment" to reporters gives an impression of guilt. Do talk to the media, but state only facts and give no opinions. Giving information about time, number of victims, responding agencies, and so forth, is acceptable. Disclosing the identity of the victim(s) or answering questions about what you think caused the accident are not appropriate responses. Answers such as "we do not know that yet" are appropriate when you are pressed for a response. Although it may be difficult, express only facts, not feelings. Absolutely avoid statements such as "If only I had taken a different course of action."

Training

Rescue, first aid, and medical training is recommended for citizens, but required for professionals (see figure 12.2). Moreover, the training should be sanctioned, professional training. A group of well-meaning amateur scuba divers who form a search and rescue team can create liability for everyone involved—even the agency they are trying to help—if they do not have professional search and rescue training. Not only must professional responders have appropriate initial training, but also their training must be ongoing and documented. Volunteers with good intentions have cost government agencies millions of dollars because they failed to meet the professional standard of care for training and practice (Smith and Smith 1994). Volunteers who want to respond to emergencies as professionals must train, practice, and document training like professionals.

Figure 12.2 Ongoing training and documentation of the training are essential for professionals and highly recommended for amateurs.

Key Points

Citizens have a moral obligation to provide assistance when an aquatic emergency occurs, whereas professional rescuers have a legal obligation to respond. Good Samaritan statutes generally protect citizens, but not professionals, from liability. Citizens should be trained in rescue and first aid techniques, but professionals must be trained. Everyone should document emergencies well for legal protection. Everyone should follow the legal procedures of obtaining consent before providing aid to conscious victims, moving victims only when necessary, continuing care until relieved by someone with equal or greater qualifications, preserving evidence whenever possible, speaking appropriately to media personnel, and keeping rescue and first aid training current.

Epilogue

Most of the safety suggestions in this book are familiar to many people. The problem is that too many people tend to ignore the recommendations. Simply knowing what to do to avoid injury is not enough; you must apply what you know. One of my favorite definitions is that wisdom is knowledge rightly applied. One of your main tasks now is to apply the safety principles that you know and have learned from your reading. Another task is to motivate others to apply the principles.

People will perform a behavior automatically after they have repeated it enough times that it has become ingrained. The automatic performance of a behavior is called a habit. Researchers tell us that 17 to 20 successful repetitions are required to produce an automatic response. If you discipline yourself to follow each safety procedure until it becomes a habit, your effort will be rewarded with peace of mind and injury avoidance.

Another task is to remind friends and family members about safety issues. Encourage them to repeat the behavior independently until it becomes automatic. If you see yourself as a motivator rather than as a safety enforcer, others will be more likely to respond favorably. When you encourage people to act for themselves because it is in their best interest, they will usually appreciate your concern for them.

A second main task is completion of the training suggested. Take initial or renewal classes. Think about who would provide aid to you if you were injured and encourage your friends and family members to take courses also. Taking a CPR or first aid class together is a good family activity. The more remote from medical assistance your aquatic activities are, the more emergency medical training you should have.

A third main task is the acquisition and maintenance of emergency medical equipment. Obtain and familiarize yourself and those who will be participating with you with rescue and first aid equipment. Establish a schedule (I recommend a couple of holidays a year) to inventory and inspect the equipment. Replace used items promptly and repair or replace damaged equipment. Thinking of how important an item can be in a life-or-death situation should provide sufficient motivation.

The fourth and final main task is to develop and practice rescue skills. You should complete rescue training to acquire rescue ability, but you need to practice the skills with others regularly to be proficient for actual use. I cannot emphasize enough the value of rescue drills during recreational outings. An aquatic rescue drill from boat or shore can be every bit as beneficial as a fire drill at home.

The goal is the same—to save lives in an emergency. You and your family and friends need to develop, review, and rehearse an emergency action plan. When everyone knows the drill and their roles, there will be less confusion and stress in an emergency.

This is an age in which time is precious. You may be thinking that you do not have time to do everything that you are supposed to do. You wonder if you can find the time or make the time. You cannot do either, but you can take the time. If the principles that are essential require time and money and you think that you cannot afford either, remember that the life of a love one is beyond value. Consider how much time legal proceedings can consume. Everything is a matter of priority. If you live near the water, own a swimming pool, go boating or fishing, or engage in family recreational activities on or about the water, you need to prevent aquatic emergencies and be prepared for them. When you make prevention and preparation a priority for yourself, your friends, and your family, you will find the time and money to fulfill the requirements. You know the goal and you know how to reach it. Now all you have to do is begin the journey one step at a time. You will be richly rewarded in unexpected ways when you do all that you can to make water your friend and not allow it to become an enemy to you or your loved ones.

Appendix A

Training Organizations

Scuba Diving

National Association of Underwater Instructors (NAUI)
9942 Currie Davis Drive, Suite H
Tampa, FL 33619
800-553-NAUI

Professional Association of Diving Instructors (PADI)
1251 East Dyer Road, #100
Santa Ana, CA 92705
949-540-7234

Scuba Schools International (SSI)
2619 Canton Court
Fort Collins, CO 80525
970-482-0883

YMCA National Scuba Program
5825-2A Live Oak Parkway
Norcross, GA 30093
770-662-5172

Handicapped Scuba Association (HSA)
1104 El Prado
San Clemente, CA 92672
949-498-6128

National Association for Cave Diving (NACD)
Post Office Box 14492
Gainesville, FL 32604
352-877-8196

First Aid and CPR

American Heart Association
7272 Greenville Avenue
Dallas, TX 75231
214-373-6300

From *Aquatic Rescue and Safety* by Dennis K. Graver, 2004, Champaign, IL: Human Kinetics.

American Red Cross
8111 Gatehouse Road
Falls Church, VA 22042
703-206-7412

National Safety Council
1121 Spring Lake Drive
Itasca, IL 60143
800-621-6244

Boating

United States Foundation for Boating Safety
880 South Prickett Street
Alexandria, VA 22304
800-336-2628

United States Power Squadron
1504 Blue Ridge Road
Raleigh, NC 27607
919-821-0281

Personal Watercraft Industry Association
200 East Randolph Drive, Suite 5100
Chicago, IL 60601
312-946-6200

United States Coast Guard
Navigation Center
7323 Telegraph Road
Alexandria, VA 22315
800-368-5647

United States Coast Guard Boating Safety Courses
800-336-BOAT

Pools and Spas

National Spa and Pool Institute
2111 Eisenhower Avenue
Alexandria, VA 22314
703-838-0083

National Swimming Pool Foundation
10803 Gulfdale, Suite 300
San Antonio, TX 78216
210-525-1227

From *Aquatic Rescue and Safety* by Dennis K. Graver, 2004, Champaign, IL: Human Kinetics.

Appendix **B**

Recommended First Aid Equipment

Standard first aid kit

Advanced first aid reference book

Small trauma dressings (new sanitary napkins)

Large trauma dressings (new diapers)

Trauma shears (for cutting exposure suits and wet clothing)

Rescue breathing mask

Manual suctioning device (for clearing airway)

Formable splint

Hypothermic thermometer

Pen and notepad

Vinegar (for marine life stings)

Chemical heat packs (for warming oxygen and victims)

Chemical cold packs (for sprains, strains, and fractures)

Two adult doses of activated charcoal (for poisoning)

Sterile water (for rinsing wounds, burns, eyes)

Medications: prescription, nonprescription, and antibiotic ointment

Antiseptic towelettes

Several towels (for drying wet victims and general use)

Several emergency blankets (disposable types)

Mylar or wool cap (for hypothermic victim)

Duct tape (multiple uses)

Flashlights with spare batteries and bulbs

Radio or cell phone for emergency communications

Local emergency contact information

Additional equipment for remote locations

Oxygen delivery system with spare cylinder

Spinal immobilization board with head blocks and straps

From *Aquatic Rescue and Safety* by Dennis K. Graver, 2004, Champaign, IL: Human Kinetics.

Aquatic Hazard Analysis

1. Rate each of the following hazards on a scale of 1 to 10 with 10 being the greatest risk.

Entry area   _____

Depth   _____

Water temperature   _____

Water clarity   _____

Bottom composition   _____

Obstructions   _____

Entanglements   _____

Currents   _____

Waves   _____

Altitude   _____

2. Rate each of the following resources on a scale of 1 to 10 with 10 being the ideal situation.

Vehicle access to area   _____

Telephone availability   _____

Emergency equipment availability   _____

Rescue team availability   _____

EMS response time   _____

Landing zone suitability   _____

Medical center availability   _____

Recompression chamber availability   _____

Participants' aquatic skills   _____

Participants' medical skills   _____

No matter how high the rating total is for section 2, the risk is too great if any of the items in section 1 are rated high. The reason is that all of the items in section 2 relate to rescue, first aid, and medical care after an accident has occurred. If any risk is great, go to a better location.

From *Aquatic Rescue and Safety* by Dennis K. Graver, 2004, Champaign, IL: Human Kinetics.

Emergency Action Plan

1. *Know in advance*

- The exact location
- Contact information (your radio frequency and call letters or phone number and local emergency contact frequencies and phone numbers)
- Your vessel identification number
- How to rescue and how to provide first aid and CPR

2 *Survey the situation*

- Look for potential hazards to rescuers.
- Determine the number of victims (does the victim have a buddy?).
- Obtain information from bystanders.
- Quickly evaluate resources—equipment and personnel.

3. *Quickly formulate a plan of action*

- Assign spotters to pinpoint the victim's exact location.
- Assign one or two bystanders to summon emergency assistance.
- Assign one person to prepare the emergency equipment.
- Assign one or two participants to prepare to extricate the victim at the exit point.
- Initiate rescue actions.

4. *Rescue the victim*

- If possible, shout encouragement to the victim.
- If possible, extend an object to the victim (reach).
- If possible, throw a rescue rope or flotation device to the victim (throw).
- If possible, use a boat to rescue the victim (row).
- As a last resort and if trained and equipped, enter the water and rescue the victim (go).

From *Aquatic Rescue and Safety* by Dennis K. Graver, 2004, Champaign, IL: Human Kinetics.

5. Assess the victim

- Provide flotation to a conscious, breathing victim.
- If the victim is not breathing and can be removed from the water quickly, expedite a rescue exit.
- If the victim is not breathing and cannot be removed from the water quickly, initiate aquatic rescue breathing while moving the victim to the exit point.
- Consider possible spinal cord injury.

6. Remove the victim from the water

- Consider spinal cord injury, water temperature, length of time without breathing, and victim's age and physical size.
- Determine the best way to extricate the victim (horizontal, if possible).
- Handle the victim as gently as possible while expediting the exit.

7. Initiate first aid

- Assess airway, breathing, and circulation and begin rescue breathing or CPR as needed.
- Have others gently cut away the victim's clothing, dry the person, and provide first aid for hypothermia.
- If possible, give heated oxygen to the victim.

8. Record medical information

- Whenever possible, prepare a written document for emergency medical personnel.
- Include a brief description of what happened, the extent of the injury, the actions taken, and the victim's response to the care provided.
- Include the victim's name, date of birth (if known), and medical conditions (if known).
- If possible, include family contact information.

9. Consider designating bystanders to do the following

- Keep observers at a distance
- Meet and direct emergency medical personnel
- Provide lighting for victim care
- Record information
- Help move or position the victim (if needed)

From *Aquatic Rescue and Safety* by Dennis K. Graver, 2004, Champaign, IL: Human Kinetics.

Appendix **E**

Recommended Readings

Associated Press. 2000. Submerged 45 minutes, canoeing victim revived. *The Everett (Wash.) Herald*, 18 April, p. 3B.

Auerbach, P. 1996. Water submersion incidents. *Dive Training* (November): 53-6.

Bjorhus, J. 1995. Bittersweet lesson—rescue puts life in perspective. *The Everett (Wash.) Herald*, 23 November, sec. A20, p. 1.

Brooks, J. 1988. Near drowning. *Pediatrics in Review* 10 (July): 5-10.

Chochinov, A., B. Baydock, G. Bristow, and G. Giesbrecht. 1998. Recovery of a 62-year-old man from prolonged cold water submersion. *Annals of Emergency Medicine* 31 (1): 127-31.

Cruikshank, B., M. Eliason, and B. Merrifield. 1988. Long-term sequelae of cold water near-drowning. *Journal of Pediatric Psychology* 13 (3): 379-88.

DeNicola, L., J. Falk, M. Swanson, M. Gayle, and N. Kissoon. 1997. Submersion injuries in children and adults. *Critical Care Clinics* 13 (3): 477-501.

Gonzalez-Rothi, R. 1987. Near drowning: Consensus and controversies in pulmonary and cerebral resuscitation. *Heart & Lung* 16 (5) (September): 474-82.

Graver, D. 1984. Rescue technique. *Skin Diver Magazine* (September): 96-8.

Graver, D. 1994. A review of aquatic rescue breathing techniques. *Sources* (July/August): 43-4.

Lippmann, J., and S. Bugg. 1991. *The DAN emergency handbook*. Carnegie, Victoria, Australia: J.L. Publications.

Martin, T. 1984. Near drowning and cold water immersion. *Annals of Emergency Medicine* 13 (4): 263-73.

National Children's Center for Rural and Agricultural Health and Safety. 1999. Rural Youth Drowning: Fact Sheet. Available: http://research.marshfieldclinic.org/children/resources/drowning/factsheet.htm. [Retrieved June 17, 2003].

Oakes, D., J. Sherck, J. Maloney, and A. Charters. 1982. Prognosis and management of victims of near-drowning. *The Journal of Trauma* 22 (7): 544-9.

Orlowski, J. 1987. Drowning, near-drowning, and ice-water submersions. *Pediatric Clinics of North America* 34 (1): 75-92.

Orlowski, J., M. Abulleil, and J. Phillips. 1987. Effects of tonicities of saline solutions on pulmonary injury in drowning. *Critical Care Medicine* 15 (2): 126-30.

Orlowski, J., M. Abulleil, and J. Phillips. 1989. The hemodynamic and cardiovascular effects of near-drowning in hypotonic, isotonic, or hypertonic solutions. *Annals of Emergency Medicine* 18 (10): 1044-9.

Pruessner, H., G. Zenner, and N. Hansel. 1988. Management of the near-drowning victim. *American Family Physician* 37 (5): 251-60.

Rinke, C. 1986. The resuscitation of near-drowning victims. *Journal of the American Medical Association* 256 (1): 75-7.

Ryan, R. 1990. Supine is fine. *Sources* (January/February): 53.

Shaw, K., and D. Briede. 1989. Submersion injuries: Drowning and near-drowning. *Emergency Medicine Clinics of North America* 7 (2): 355-70.

From *Aquatic Rescue and Safety* by Dennis K. Graver, 2004, Champaign, IL: Human Kinetics.

Shepherd, S. 1989. Immersion injury: Drowning and near drowning. *Drowning* 85 (8): 183-91.

Shovein, J. 1989. Near-drowning. *Journal of Nursing* (May): 680-6.

Stevick, E. 1994. To the rescue. *The Everett (Wash.) Herald*, 2 September.

Washington State Department of Health. 1998. Childhood injury prevention. Olympia, WA: Washington State Department of Health.

Wilmshurst, P., M. Nuri, A. Crowther, and M. Webb-Peploe. 1984. Recurrent pulmonary edema in scuba divers; prodrome of hypertension: A new syndrome. *Proceedings of the 8th Symposium on Underwater Physiology*. Bethesda, MD: Undersea Medical Society, 327-39.

Wintemute, G. 1990. Childhood drowning and near-drowning in the United States. *American Journal of Disease in Childhood* 144 (June): 663-9.

References

American Heart Association. 1999. *Heart and stroke facts.* Dallas: American Heart Association.

American Heart Association. 2000. *Guidelines 2000 for cardiopulmonary resuscitation and emergency cardiovascular care.* Dallas: American Heart Association.

American Trauma Society. 2001. *Guide to water safety.* Marlboro, MD: American Trauma Society.

Arborelius, M., U.I. Balldin, B. Lilja, C.E.G. Lundgren. 1972. Hemodynamic changes in man during immersion with the head above water. *Aerospace Medicine* 43: 592-8.

Bachrach, J., and G. Egstrom. 1990. *Conference precedings of the 1990 American Academy of Underwater Sciences.* American Academy of Underwater Sciences, Tampa, Florida.

Baker, S.P., B. O'Neill, and R.S. Karpf. 1984. *The injury fact book.* Lexington, MA: D.C. Heath and Company.

British Sub-Aqua Club. 1987. *Safety and rescue for divers.* London: Stanley Paul.

Children's Hospital and Medical Center. 1992. *Water safety: A parent's guide for children and teens.* Seattle: Children's Hospital and Medical Center.

Divers Alert Network. 2001. *Report on decompression illness, diving fatalities and project dive exploration.* Durham, NC: Divers Alert Network.

Dueker, C., and C. Brown, eds. 1999. *Near drowning workshop proceedings.* Kensington, MD: Undersea and Hyperbaric Medical Society.

Edmonds, C. 1998. Drowning syndromes: The mechanism. *SPUMS Journal* 28 (1): 2-9.

Evans, C. 1999. Think safety at the swimming pool and beach. *National Safety Council* (Summer): 8-9.

Gabrielli, A., and J. Layon. 1997. Drowning and near drowning. *Journal of Florida Medical Association* 84 (7): 452-7.

Golden, F., G. Hervey, and M. Tipton. 1991. Circum-rescue collapse: Collapse, sometimes fatal, associated with rescue of immersion victims. *Journal of the Royal Naval Medical Service* 77: 139-49.

Golden, F., M. Tipton, and R. Scott. 1997. Immersion, near-drowning and drowning. *British Journal of Anesthesia* 79: 214-25.

Goode, R.C., J. Duffin, and R. Miller. 1975. Sudden cold water immersion. *Respiration Physiology* 23: 301.

Graver, D. 1995. Northwest Diving Rescue Workshops.

Graver, D. 1999. *Scuba diving.* Champaign, IL: Human Kinetics.

Harpur, G.D. 1974. Ninety second deep scuba rescue. *NAUI News* (January): 4-8.

Heimlich, H. 1981. Subdiaphragmatic pressure to expel water from the lungs of drowning persons. *Annals of Emergency Medicine* 10: 9.

Jacobs, M. 1998. *Drowning, near drowning, and cold water immersion.* Diver's Alert Network Dive Medicine Workshop, April 29-May 2, Cozumel, Mexico.

Joki, E., and L. Melzer. 1971. Acute fatal nontraumatic collapse during work and sport. *Exercise and Cardiac Death: Medicine and Sport*, Vol. 5. Basle, Switzerland: Darger.

Keating, W.R., and M.G. Hayward. 1981. Sudden death in cold water and ventricular arryhthmia. *Journal of Forensic Science* 26: 459.

King County EMS. 2000. Competency-Based Training 350. Seattle: King County EMS.

Limmer, D., M. O'Keefe, H. Grant, R. Murray, J. Bergeron, B. Adams, and E. Dickinson. 2001. *Emergency Care*. 9th ed. Upper Saddle River, NJ: Brady/Prentice Hall.

McDonough, J., J. Barutt, and J. Saffron. 1989. *Cardiac arrythmias as a precursor to drowning accidents*. Undersea and Hyperbaric Medical Society Chapter Meeting report.

Mistovich, J., B. Hafen, K. Karren, and H. Werman. 2000. *Prehospital emergency care*. 6th ed. Upper Saddle River, NJ: Brady/Prentice Hall.

Modell, J. 1971. *The pathophysiology and treatment of drowning and near drowning*. Springfield, IL: Charles C Thomas.

Modell, J. 1976. Clinical course of 91 consecutive near-drowning victims. *Chest* 70: 231.

National Institute on Alcohol Abuse and Alcoholism. 1981. *Alcohol and health*. Rockville, MD: Smith & Smith.

National SAFE Kids Campaign. n.d. Promoting child safety to prevent unintentional injury. Available: http://www.safekids.org/tier3_cd.cfm?content_item_id=1032&folder_id=540. [Retrieved June 10, 2003].

National Safety Council. 1997. *Advanced first aid*. Sudbury, MA: Jones and Bartlett.

National Safety Council. 2001. *Injury facts*. Itasca, IL: National Safety Council.

National Transportation Safety Board. 1993. *Recreational boating safety, safety study*. Washington, DC: National Transportation Safety Board.

Orlowski, J. 1982. Submersion accidents in children with epilepsy. *American Journal for Disabled Children* 136: 777-80.

Orlowski, J. 1987. Vomiting as a complication of the Heimlich Maneuver. *Journal of the American Medical Association* 258: 512-3.

Orlowski, J. 1988. Drowning, near-drowning, and ice-water drowning. *Journal of the American Medical Association* 260 (3): 390-1.

Ornato, J. 1986. The resuscitation of near-drowning victims. *Journal of the American Medical Association* 256 (1): 75-7.

Patetta, M., P. Biddinger, J. Freeman, and J. MacCormack. 1986. Current trends North Carolina drownings. *Morbidity and Mortality Weekly Report* 35: 635-8.

Pia, F. 1974. Observations on the drowning of non-swimmers. *Journal of Physical Education* 71 (6): 164-7.

Pierce, A. 1985. *Scuba life saving*. Champaign, IL: Leisure Press.

Professional Association of Diving Instructors. 1985. *PADI rescue diver manual*. Santa Ana, CA: Professional Association of Diving Instructors.

Quan, L., E. Gore, K. Wentz, J. Allen, and A. Novack. 1989. Ten-year study of pediatric drownings and near-drownings in King County, Washington: Lessons in injury prevention. *Pediatrics* 83 (6): 1035-40.

Royal Lifesaving Society of Canada. 1990. *Drowning and water related deaths in Alberta—1990*. Alberta: Royal Lifesaving Society of Canada.

Seley, C. 1980. Physiological changes during scuba diving. *NAUI News* (August/September): 9.

Shepherd, J., and P. Vanhoutte. 1979. *The human cardiovascular system: Facts and concepts*. New York: Raven Press.

Smith, D., and S. Smith. 1994. *Water rescue*. St. Louis: Mosby-Year Book.

Spinal Cord Injury Information Network. 2001. Spinal cord injury: Facts and figures at a glance. Available: http//www.spinalcord.uab.edu/show.asp?durki=21446. [Retrived June 10, 2003].

Spyker, D. 1985. Submersion injury epidemiology, prevention and management. *Pediatric Clinics of North America* 32 (1): 113-25.

Surawicz, B. 1985. Ventricular fibrillation. *Journal of American College of Cardiology* 5 (6): 43b-54b.

U.S. Centers for Disease Control. 1985. *Drownings in the U.S., 1985.* Atlanta: U.S. Centers for Disease Control.

U.S. Consumer Product Safety Commission. 1994a. *Guidelines for entrapment hazards: Making pools and spas safer.* Publication #363. Washington, DC: U.S. Consumer Product Safety Commission.

U.S. Consumer Product Safety Commission. 1994b. *How to plan for the unexpected: Preventing child drownings.* Publication #359. Washington, DC: U.S. Consumer Product Safety Commission.

U.S. Consumer Product Safety Commission. 1994c. *Spas, hot tubs, and whirlpools.* Consumer Product Safety Alert. Washington, DC: U.S. Consumer Product Safety Commission.

Weinstein, M., and B. Krieger. 1996. Near-drowning: Epidemiology, pathophysiology, and initial treatment. *Journal of Emergency Medicine* 14 (4): 461-7.

Wilmshurst, P., M. Nuri, A. Crowther, and M. Webb-Peploe. 1989. Cold-induced pulmonary edema in scuba divers and swimmers and subsequent development of hypertension. *The Lancet* 14 (January): 62-5.

Index

Note: The italicized *f* or *t* following a page number denote a figure or table on that page, respectfully. The italicized *ff* or *tt* following a page number denotes multiple figures or tables on that page.

About the Author

Photo courtesy of James Beckett

Dennis Graver has worked in aquatics for more than 25 years as a water rescue and scuba diving instructor. He is an emergency medical technician (EMT) and a senior EMS instructor, and he has current instructor training ratings for first aid, oxygen first aid, and scuba. He is a member of the National Association of Underwater Instructors (NAUI), Professional Association of Dive Instructors (PADI), the Handicapped Scuba Association, the Undersea and Hyperbaric Medical Society, the Academy of Underwater Arts and Sciences, the Diver's Alert Network, and the Underwater Society of America. He is an active volunteer firefighter and EMT, district medical officer, and district CPR training coordinator for his local fire district.

Graver has authored 30 books and manuals including *Scuba Diving* and *Scuba Diving First Aid*. He has also contributed hundreds of articles to such magazines as *Skin Diver*, *Sources*, and *Undercurrents* as well as several NAUI technical publications.

He has won numerous awards including the Underwater Society of America Sports Education award, Outstanding EMS Instructor award, and NAUI Outstanding Contribution to Diving award. He has been an underwater photographer since 1970 and has been repeatedly recognized by the Underwater Photographic Society, and his photos have graced the covers of many magazines and illustrated several diving texts and audiovisual educational programs.

Graver has greatly influenced scuba diving with his development of a dive table multilevel diving technique for recreational diving and a breathing mask technique for diving rescue. He also has designed the NAUI Dive Time Calculator and the first PADI dive tables.

Graver is currently a member of the Undersea Medical Society, NAUI, the Handicapped Scuba Association, and the Divers Alert Network. Dennis and his wife, Barbara, reside in Camano Island, Washington.

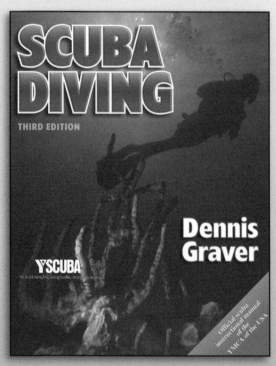